GREAT SPORTS TEAMS

THE CHICAGO WHITE SOX

JOHN F. GRABOWSKI

LUCENT BOOKS®

THOMSON
GALE

San Diego • Detroit • New York • San Francisco • Cleveland
New Haven, Conn. • Waterville, Maine • London • Munich

THOMSON

━━━━━✳━━━━━™

GALE

Cover photo: Jim Parque readies to release his devastating fastball.

LIBRARY OF CONGRESS CATALOGING-IN-PUBLICATION DATA

Grabowski, John F.
   Chicago White Sox / by John F. Grabowski.
     v. cm. — (Great sports teams)
Includes bibliographical references and index.
Summary: Discusses the relationship of Chicago to the formation of The Chicago White
Sox with profiles of: Joe Jackson, Nellie Fox, Minnie Minoso, Bill Veeck, Dick Allen, and
Frank Thomas.
Contents: Second-class citizens in the second city—The Comiskey curse—Joe Jackson—
Nellie Fox—Minnie Minoso—Bill Veeck—Dick Allen—Frank Thomas.
   ISBN 1-56006-938-4 (alk. paper)
   1. Chicago White Sox (Baseball team)—History—Juvenile literature. 2. Baseball players—
United States—Biography—Juvenile literature. [1. Chicago White Sox (Baseball team)—
History.] I. Title. II. Great sports teams (Lucent Books)
   GV875.C58 G73 2003
   796.357'64'0977311—dc21

                                            2002009469

Printed in the United States of America

Contents

FOREWORD

Former Supreme Court Chief Justice Warren Burger once said he always read the sports section of the newspaper first because it was about humanity's successes, while the front page listed only humanity's failures. Millions of people across the country today would probably agree with Burger's preference for tales of human endurance, record-breaking performances, and feats of athletic prowess. Although these accomplishments are far beyond what most Americans can ever hope to achieve, average people, the fans, do want to affect what happens on the field of play. Thus, their role becomes one of encouragement. They cheer for their favorite players and team and boo the opposition.

ABC Sports president Roone Arledge once attempted to explain the relationship between fan and team. Sport, said Arledge, is "a set of created circumstances—artificial circumstances—set up to frustrate a man in pursuit of a goal. He has to have certain skills to overcome those obstacles—or even to challenge them. And people who don't have those skills cheer him and admire him." Over a period of time, the admirers may develop a rabid—even irrational—allegiance to a particular team. Indeed, the word "fan" itself is derived from the word "fanatic," someone possessed by an excessive and irrational zeal. Sometimes this devotion to a team is because of a favorite player; often it's because of where a person lives, and, occasionally, it's because of a family allegiance to a particular club.

Whatever the reason, the bond formed between team and fan often defies reason. It may be easy to understand the appeal of the New York Yankees, a team that has gone to the World Series an incredible thirty-eight times and won twenty-six championships, nearly three times as many as any other major league baseball team. It is more difficult, though, to comprehend the fanaticism of Chicago Cubs fans, who faithfully follow the progress of a team that hasn't won a World Series since 1908. Regardless, the Cubs have surpassed the 2 million mark in home attendance in fourteen of the last seventeen years. In fact, their two highest totals were posted in 1999 and 2000, when the team finished in last place.

Each volume in Lucent's Great Sports Teams series examines a team that has left its mark on the "American sports consciousness." Each book looks at the history and tradition of the club in an attempt to understand its appeal and the loyalty —even passion—of its fans. Each volume also examines the lives and careers of people who played significant roles in the team's history. Players, managers, coaches, and front-office executives are represented.

Endnoted quotations help bring the text in each book to life. In addition, all books include an annotated bibliography and a For Further Reading list to supply students with sources for conducting additional individual research.

No one volume can hope to explain fully the mystique of the New York Yankees, Boston Celtics, Dallas Cowboys, or Montreal Canadiens. The Lucent Great Sports Teams series, however, gives interested readers a solid start on the road to understanding the mysterious bond that exists between modern professional sports teams and their devoted followers.

Second-Class Citizens in the Second City

As one of the nation's largest cities, Chicago is one of the few capable of supporting more than one major-league baseball team. For most of their history, however, the White Sox have been second in popularity to the Cubs, their neighbors on the city's North Side. Despite this, the White Sox have managed to survive for more than a century, a testimony to the loyalty of their fans.

The City Series

The competitiveness that exists between the two teams was perhaps best seen in the postseason City Series, a set of exhibition games played between the two clubs from 1903 to 1942 to determine the city's unofficial champion. Of the twenty-five competitions held over that period, eighteen were won by the White Sox, six by the Cubs, and one ended in a tie.

White Sox domination (they won the final eight series played) eventually resulted in a drop in interest (since there was less doubt about the outcome of the game) and attendance declined. When several players from the two teams enlisted in the service during World War II, interest waned even more as the quality of play deteriorated. The Series was finally discontinued after the 1942 matchup.

The Drought

For Chicagoans annually frustrated in their quest for a championship, the City Series was their World Series. The last time the White Sox won the World Series was back in 1917. They have not won a pennant since 1959. The Cubs, their neighbors to the north, have gone even longer without a title of some sort, their last pennant coming in 1945 and their last championship more than ninety years ago in 1908.

Although the White Sox are more often than not the stronger of the two teams, the Cubs generally draw better at the gate. Reasons given for this usually center on the attractiveness of Wrigley Field with its ivy-covered walls as a venue for watching ball games. The crowds at Wrigley seem to have more fun rooting for losers than do those at Comiskey Park. The location of Wrigley in

White Sox shortstop Ozzie Guillen slides into home plate ahead of the throw. The Sox have struggled throughout their 102-year history to produce winning seasons.

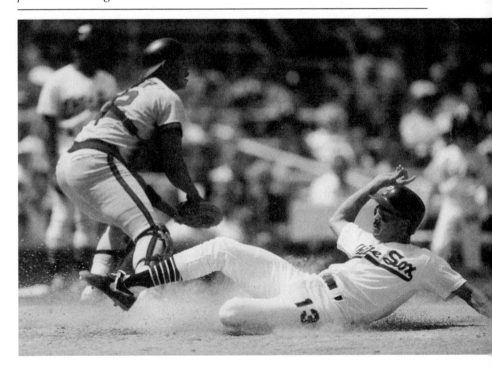

a part of town where millions of fans can walk up to the gates makes it more accessible than Comiskey, which is located in a comparatively desolate industrial area. Even the weather seems to be a factor, with "White Sox weather" referring to the dreary, overcast skies that seem more prevalent at Comiskey.

When everything is taken into account, it is easy to see why former owner Bill Veeck once said, "If there is any justice in this world, to be a White Sox fan frees a man from any other form of penance."[1] Through it all, Sox fans have remained faithful to their team. Though they may be considered second-class citizens in Chicago, White Sox fans are truly first-class fans in a first-class sports town.

CHAPTER 1

The Comiskey Curse

In over a century of play in the American League, the Chicago White Sox have given their fans little reason to brag about their team. They have won just a pair of World Series titles, and their most famous teams have been the Hitless Wonders of the early part of the century and the Black Sox of 1919, remembered for throwing the World Series to the Cincinnati Reds. Their lack of success has been blamed on many things, including what is sometimes referred to as the Comiskey Curse. Even though the Sox have rarely been consistent winners, however, they are usually entertaining. The Go-Go Sox, Bill Veeck, Joe Jackson, Luis Aparicio, Frank Thomas, and others have kept loyal Chicago fans coming out in support of one of the league's oldest franchises.

A New Team for Chicago

Major league baseball in the late nineteenth century was in a state of flux. Although the National League had been in existence since 1876, there were challenges over the years from the American Association (1882–91), the Union Association (1884), and the Players' League (1890). And another league would soon take shape. In 1893, former sportswriter Byron Bancroft "Ban" Johnson took

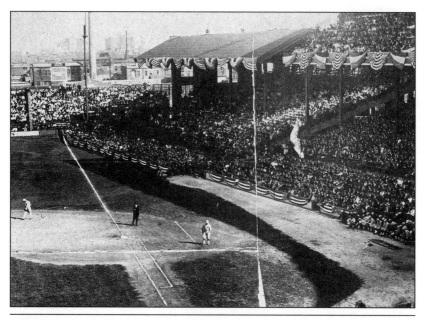

The grandstands of Comiskey Park are packed for a 1919 World Series game between the Chicago White Sox and Cincinnati Reds. The most famous scandal in baseball history erupted when it was rumored that Chicago threw the Series.

over as president of a struggling minor-league baseball circuit known as the Western League. Under Johnson's shrewd leadership, the league soon became a financial success. At the league's annual meeting in October 1899, Johnson revealed his plan to expand east and eventually gain status as a second major league. The circuit's name was officially changed to the American League of Professional Ball Clubs to symbolize its proposed expansion.

During the initial expansion, the National League (NL) approved the move of the American League's St. Paul Saints franchise to Chicago on three conditions, as set forth by James Hart, owner of the NL's Chicago Orphans (Cubs). First, the team had to be situated south of Thirty-fifth Street (the Chicago club of the National League drew from fans on the city's North Side). Second, the club could not use the name Chicago. Finally, the team had to give the more established franchise the right to draft two of its players every year.

Johnson and Saints' owner Charles Comiskey formally signed a one-year agreement consenting to these conditions on March 21, 1900. Having grown up in the area, Comiskey knew that the residents of the South Side neighborhood would be eager to support their own team. They got around the stipulation about using Chicago in their name by nicknaming their club the White Stockings. That had been the original name of the National League team, and was still associated with Chicago in the minds of sports fans.

With the American League (AL) still considered a minor league, the White Stockings won the 1900 pennant under manager Comiskey. The team played its home games at South Side Park, a former cricket field at Thirty-ninth Street and Wentworth Avenue. That winter, Johnson decided against signing an extension of the agreement. He drafted a 140-game schedule and declared the American League to be a major league.

On April 24, 1901, the White Stockings played the first official American League game (as a major league) and defeated the Cleveland Blues (Indians) by a score of 8–2. Chicago's season was a rousing success, despite the predictions of James Hart. ("They may talk all they want about the city supporting two teams," he had warned, "but they are mistaken. Chicago can only support *one* Chicago club!"[2]) Paced by manager and star pitcher Clark Griffith's twenty-four victories, the White Stockings took the pennant and, just as important, outdrew their National League counterparts by nearly 150,000 fans.

The Hitless Wonders

Following the 1902 season, Johnson asked Griffith to leave Chicago to take over as manager of the New York franchise that was to begin play in 1903. Comiskey named outfielder/pitcher Nixey Callahan (who had hurled the first no-hitter in franchise history in 1902) as the team's new manager. Callahan's penchant for drinking and fighting soon grew tiresome, however, and he was replaced by outfielder Fielder Jones after less than a season and a half at the helm.

Jones proved to be a far better choice. After bringing the team home in third place in 1904 and in second the next season, he led the White Sox to the pennant in 1906. (The *Chicago Tribune* had shortened the team's name to White Sox for headline-writing purposes.) The high spot of the season was a major-league-record nineteen-game winning streak (since broken) that the team put together in August.

The club became known as the Hitless Wonders because of its weak hitting. Chicago's team batting average was a woeful .230, with a slugging average not much higher. Pitching was the team's strong point, with Frank Owen, Nick Altrock, Doc White, and Ed Walsh each winning seventeen or more games.

All eyes turned to Chicago at World Series time. In what was termed the Trolley Car Series, the Sox's opponents were none other than their crosstown neighbors, the Orphans. (The team would not become known as the Cubs until the following season.) The mighty Orphans were heavy favorites, having won a major-league-record 116 games during the regular season. In the only all-Chicago World Series of the century, however, the Sox showed how good pitching could stop good hitting. Jones's crew held the National League champions to a .196 batting average and won four of six games to take the title. (The White Sox themselves hit just two points higher.)

In the clubhouse celebration after the final game, Chicago owner Comiskey handed Jones a check for $15,000 and told him to divide it among the players. It was a surprising gesture from a man who was not known to throw money around. It became more understandable some weeks later when Comiskey told the team that the "bonus" was also their raise for the new season. The move created dissension on the club and added to Comiskey's reputation for being tightfisted.

The White Sox managed to be competitive again in 1908 despite an offense that was even more ineffectual than the year before. The team batted only .224 and hit a grand total of three home runs all season. Jones kept them in the pennant race until the last day of the regular season. The team was carried by the amazing pitching of Big Ed Walsh. Walsh put together one of the greatest seasons ever by a pitcher. He won an incredible forty games (including eleven shutouts) while compiling an earned run average of 1.42 and striking out a league-leading 269 batters. Despite Walsh's heroics, Comiskey denied his request for a $7,500 salary for 1909. The denial would add to the players' growing resentment toward the owner.

A New Home and a World Series Victory

With the era of the Hitless Wonders coming to an end, the White Sox began a period of rebuilding. The most memorable event of the 1910 season was the opening of the Sox's new home field, Comiskey Park. The stadium was a pitcher's delight. Indeed, during the early phases of the park's construction, star pitcher Ed Walsh had consulted with the design engineers. His input had a significant role in determining the park's spacious dimensions since, as a pitcher, he preferred to make it harder to hit home runs.

Chicago's first concrete and steel sports stadium opened on July 1, 1910, with Walsh and the White Sox losing a 2–0 decision to the St. Louis Browns. It proved to be a harbinger of things to come. The Sox set records for batting futility that season, with a .211 batting average and .261 slugging percentage. Chicago finished in sixth place, thirty-five and a half games behind the pennant-winning Philadelphia Athletics.

Third baseman George "Buck" Weaver poses with outstretched glove in a 1918 photograph.

The White Sox would continue to struggle along until the 1915 season. The previous winter, Comiskey had purchased the contract of second baseman Eddie Collins from the Athletics. The price was not cheap. It included a $15,000 bonus and a five-year, $75,000 contract for the future Hall of Famer. Collins's deal would eventually split the team as many players resented his salary. On the field, however, the move brought immediate dividends. Collins batted .332 and stole forty-six bases in 1915. With pitchers Jim Scott and Urban "Red" Faber each winning twenty-four games, the White Sox moved up to third place in the American League standings.

That August, another trade brought slugging outfielder Joe Jackson to the club. Using the proceeds derived from Chicago's rising attendance, Comiskey continued to add key players, including outfielder Oscar "Happy" Felsch, third baseman George "Buck" Weaver, catcher Ray Schalk, and shortstop Charles "Swede" Risberg. Claude "Lefty" Williams strengthened a pitching staff that had added right-hander Eddie Cicotte in 1912.

After a second-place finish in 1916, the White Sox added the final piece of the puzzle when they obtained first baseman Arnold "Chick" Gandil from the Washington Senators prior to the start of the 1917 season. The club jelled under the leadership of Clarence "Pants" Rowland, who had taken over as manager in December 1914. The Sox raced to the top of the standings and cruised to the pennant, winning a franchise-record one hundred games in the process. Jackson batted .351 and drove home ninety-six runs to lead the team in hitting, while Cicotte won twenty-nine games and Williams twenty-three to pace the pitching staff.

In the World Series that year, Eddie Collins batted .409 to lead the club to victory over the New York Giants in six games. In one of the most famous moments in Series history, Collins scored what proved to be the winning run in the final contest when he was chased across an unguarded home plate by New York third baseman Heinie Zimmerman.

Team portrait of the 1917 World Champion White Sox. On their way to winning a first World Series title, the team won a franchise-record one hundred games.

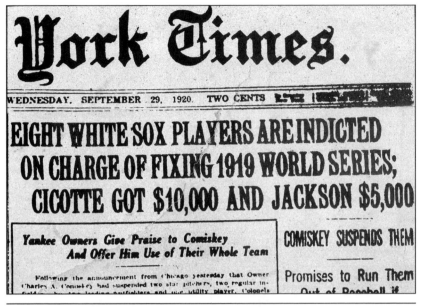

The headlines of the September 29, 1920, edition of the New York Times *report the indictment of eight Chicago White Sox players charged with fixing the 1919 World Series.*

The Black Sox Scandal

Several Chicago players went to serve their nation in World War I in 1918, and the team dropped to sixth place. The White Sox returned to full strength the following season. Under new manager William "Kid" Gleason, the team won its second flag in three years in a close pennant race. The Sox moved on to the World Series, where they were heavy favorites to defeat the National League–champion Cincinnati Redlegs.

It surprised everyone, therefore, when the Reds won the first two games of the best-of-nine Series (the first of three years in which nine games were played instead of seven). Immediately after the first loss, Comiskey approached Ban Johnson and National League president John Heydler with his suspicions that something about the Series was amiss. His comments were dismissed, however, as being nothing more than the complaints of a sore loser. The Reds proceeded to shock the baseball world by defeating the White Sox, five games to three.

Swede Risberg (left), Buck Weaver (center) and Happy Felsch (right) wait outside a courtroom with their attorneys during the Black Sox scandal.

Rumors of a possible fix became more widespread in the winter months and into the 1920 season. A special Cook County grand jury finally convened to look into allegations of crookedness in baseball. On September 29, Cicotte and Jackson admitted to having received money from Claude Williams to throw Series games and implicated Williams, Felsch, Gandil, Risberg, Weaver, and reserve infielder Fred McMullin. Comiskey immediately suspended the eight players.

At the time, there were no laws in Illinois covering fixing games. The players were brought up on charges of conspiring to defraud the public and injure the business of Charles Comiskey and the American League. The trial began in July 1921. The nebulous charges were difficult to prove, and the players were eventually acquitted on August 2, when transcripts of Cicotte's and Jackson's testimony mysteriously disappeared. The next day, however, newly named baseball commissioner Judge Kenesaw Mountain Landis banished them from the game. "Regardless of the verdict of juries," said Landis, "no player who throws a ball game, no player that undertakes or promises to throw a ball game, no player that sits in conference with a bunch of crooked players and gamblers where the ways and means of throwing a game are discussed and does not promptly tell his club about it, will ever play professional baseball."[3] The 1919 White Sox team would forever be remembered as the Black Sox in the darkest hour in major-league baseball history.

The Worst of Times

Although Comiskey's miserliness in his dealings with his players was the motivation for their actions, the fans, in general, did not hold him responsible. With the disgraced eight gone from the roster, Comiskey turned to discarded veterans and untested rookies to take their place. The club dropped to seventh place in 1921 and began a stretch of fifteen consecutive years in the second division.

During this time, Chicago players were involved in a series of events that eventually came to be referred to as the Comiskey Curse. Although the disgraced owner was willing to spend money to bring new young ballplayers to Chicago, he still refused to pay his veterans their proper value. He denied pitcher Dickie Kerr—one of the untainted heroes of the 1919 Series for the Sox—a modest $500 raise after he won nineteen games in 1921. Kerr jumped to a sandlot team outside of organized baseball. While there he pitched against several of the Black Sox players in a semipro game. For this, he was banished from baseball for four years by Judge Landis. In 1927, center fielder Johnny Mostil attempted suicide during spring training following an affair with the wife of teammate Red Faber. Several years later, infielder Bill Cissell turned to alcohol after failing to live up to the promise he had shown as a rookie.

With the White Sox mired deep in the second division, Comiskey fell into a depression. On October 26, 1931, he passed away from the combined effects of old age and poor health. Many people believed he died from a broken heart.

Mediocrity

With Comiskey's passing, control of the team passed on to his son, Lou. The most important move made during his tenure was his first deal. Comiskey obtained outfielders Al Simmons and Mule Haas and second baseman Jimmy Dykes from the Athletics for $100,000. Dykes took over as White Sox manager in 1934 and remained in the position until 1946.

The year 1931 also saw Luke Appling installed as the White Sox shortstop. Over the next two decades, Appling would be a perennial All-Star for Chicago. He would eventually be elected to the Baseball Hall of Fame in 1964. Ted Lyons was the team's most noted pitcher during this period. He won twenty games in a season three times in his twenty-one-year career and retired with 260 victories. The pair helped the team achieve some degree of stability on the field, but success was another matter. The Sox were competitive, but rarely more than mediocre.

Ted Lyons displays perfect release at a 1933 White Sox training camp. Lyons is one of the winningest pitchers in the history of the team.

Lou Comiskey died in 1940 and control of the team eventually passed on to his widow, Grace. Leslie O'Connor, a long-time associate of Judge Landis, was named general manager in 1945 and proceeded to throw the franchise into a state of disarray. One of his moves (illegally signing a Chicago prep school player) resulted in his receiving a $500 fine. When O'Connor refused to pay, Commissioner A.B. "Happy" Chandler suspended the team from the American League ("As long as the suspension stands," warned Chandler, "the White Sox cannot ask waivers on players, claim players, sign contracts, or participate in baseball's transactions or activities."[4]) The suspension was lifted shortly afterward when the fine was paid. It was the first and only time in league history that such an action was taken.

The team reached its low point in 1948 when it lost 101 games and finished in last place. Determined to right the sinking ship, the Comiskey family brought in Frank "Trader" Lane to replace O'Connor. Lane had acquired his nickname because of his willingness to trade anyone and everyone. In seven seasons with the White Sox, he completed 155 transactions involving 220 players. Included among his best acquisitions were pitcher Billy Pierce, shortstop Chico Carrasquel, second baseman Nellie Fox, outfielder Minnie Minoso, and catcher Sherm Lollar. These players would form the core of the team that brought Chicago back to glory in the late 1950s.

The Go-Go Sox

Under new manager Paul Richards, the White Sox began on the road back to respectability in 1951. After seven straight losing seasons, the team finished in fourth place at 81–73. Chicago's offense was spearheaded by timely hitting and a trio of fleet-footed players—Carrasquel, Minoso, and outfielder Jim Busby—whose base-stealing exploits were encouraged by the fans' cries of "Go! Go! Go!" The team led the league in both batting and stolen bases.

Chicago's improvement continued through the decade, but the New York Yankees always managed to finish ahead of them. Richards left to take a position with the Baltimore Orioles in 1954, and Lane moved on to the St. Louis Cardinals the next year. Marty Marion's two-year stint as manager was deemed a disappointment, leaving the door open for former catcher Al Lopez to take over in 1957.

With speedster Luis Aparicio having teamed up at shortstop with Nellie Fox in 1956, the Sox now boasted perhaps the best keystone combination in the majors. The duo led Chicago to second-place finishes in both 1957 and 1958, giving White Sox fans renewed hope for the future. That future would be faced by new ownership. In March 1959, Bill Veeck and his partners bought the White Sox from the Comiskey family.

As the 1959 season began, Lopez shared the fans' optimism. "The Yankees can be had this year,"[5] he declared. His words proved prophetic. Led by Early Wynn's twenty-two wins, Lollar's twenty-two home runs, and Aparicio's fifty-six stolen bases, the Sox won the pennant, five games ahead of the Cleveland Indians. (The Yankees, beset by injuries, were never a factor in the race.) Although he did not lead the league in a single major category, Nellie Fox became the first White Sox player ever voted Most Valuable Player. His .306 batting average and leadership qualities proved to be invaluable. After forty frustrating years, the White Sox were back on top of the American League to the delight of their faithful fans who set a franchise attendance record.

Although no team surpassed the White Sox during the 1959 American League season, the Los Angeles Dodgers were up to the task in the World Series. Chicago won the opener, 11–0, behind a pair of Ted Kluszewski home runs, but Los Angeles bounced back to take four of the next five games for the title. Although the White Sox came up short in their bid to give the city its first World Series championship since 1917, they provided fans and players alike with many memories. As center fielder Jim Landis said, "To be a part of something like that was really special."[6]

Returning to the Pack

In hopes of bringing home another pennant in 1960, owner Veeck began trading the Sox's top prospects for experienced veterans (whose best days, unfortunately, were behind them). Norm Cash, John Romano, Johnny Callison, Earl Battey, and Don Mincher all were gone before May even began. The result was a club that remained competitive for much of the year before falling to third place. (Many fans thought the most exciting thing to be seen at Comiskey Park in 1960 was the exploding scoreboard installed by Veeck at a cost of $350,000.)

Suffering from various physical ailments, Veeck put the team up for sale the next season. It was purchased by a group headed by Arthur C. Allyn Jr. In August, Ed Short took over as general manager and began ridding the club of many of its veterans. He continued the overhaul over the next couple of seasons. In January 1963, Luis Aparicio, a fan favorite who had led the American League in stolen bases in each of his seven seasons with the Sox, was dealt to Baltimore. The angry shortstop showed his displeasure by placing a curse on the club. Said Aparicio, "The Sox will need 40 years to win the pennant again!"[7] To the dismay of White Sox fans, his words have proven to be prophetic.

After three consecutive second-place finishes in 1963, 1964, and 1965, Chicago saw its string of seventeen consecutive first-division finishes end in 1968. That year, the club fell to eighth place under manager Eddie Stanky, whose combative nature had created increasing dissension on the team. With attendance on the decline, rumors began to spread that owner Allyn was considering moving the franchise to Milwaukee. The Sox played ten "home" games there in 1968, and to many the move seemed imminent.

The next year, however, Allyn had the opportunity to sell the club to a group that wanted a team for Milwaukee. After realizing how negatively his public image would be affected if the move was made, he decided instead to sell his interests to his brother John, who was committed to keeping the team in Chicago and restoring the club to its former glory.

The Long Road Back

In the first year of John Allyn's tenure, the White Sox lost a franchise-record 106 games and finished 42 games behind the Western Division–leading Minnesota Twins. Allyn brought in Stuart Holcomb to head baseball operations. Holcomb signed Chuck Tanner as the team's new manager and Roland Hemond as director of player personnel. The new regime helped the team show a twenty-three-game improvement in 1971 as third baseman Bill Melton became the first White Sox player ever to lead the league in home runs.

During the off-season, the Sox acquired controversial slugger Dick Allen from the Los Angeles Dodgers. Allen brought immediate excitement to the team, leading the league in home runs, runs batted in, walks, and slugging percentage in 1972. The White Sox surpassed the 1 million mark in attendance for the first time in seven seasons as the team climbed to second place in the standings. For his contributions, Allen was named the league's Most Valuable Player. During the off-season, he signed a contract that made him the highest-paid player in the game.

Unfortunately, Allen soon wore out his welcome. He was resented by some of the veterans who had taken pay cuts in order to help pay for his record salary. When manager Tanner tried to enforce stiffer training rules in 1974, Allen walked out on the team. He was eventually traded to the Atlanta Braves following the 1974 season. With Allen gone, attendance again dropped. Faced with the prospect of financial ruin, Allyn had to decide whether to sell the team to a group that would move it to Seattle, or to former Chicago owner Bill Veeck. On December 10, 1975, Veeck took over the reins for the second time.

The Reinsdorf and Einhorn Years

Since Veeck's first stint as owner, free agency had changed the face of the game. Players with several years of service now had the opportunity to play out their contract and sign with the team of their choice. Since Veeck did not have the resources to go after the higher-priced free agents, he instituted a "rent-a-player" policy in which he acquired players with a year left on their contract, knowing they would leave after that one season. The plan worked in 1977 as future free agents Richie Zisk and Oscar Gamble helped the club to a third-place finish. The White Sox quickly returned to their losing ways, however, and in January 1981, Veeck finalized a deal selling the club to a partnership headed by real estate baron Jerry Reinsdorf and former television producer Eddie Einhorn.

With lawyer and former major-league infielder Tony La Russa as the Chicago manager, the Sox began their climb back to the top. Reinsdorf spent money freely to add players like Carlton Fisk and Greg Luzinski to the lineup. The result was the Sox's first Western Division title, by a resounding twenty-game margin, in

1983. Chicago's pitching and hitting collapsed the next season, however, and the team did not seriously contend for the rest of the decade.

New Comiskey

To be able to compete successfully for the Chicago fans' dollar with the crosstown Cubs, Reinsdorf sought a new ballpark for the Sox. When his plan did not immediately meet with approval, he threatened to move the team to St. Petersburg, Florida. In a last-ditch attempt to save the franchise, Illinois governor James Thompson was able to get a bill passed to fund the new stadium, and groundbreaking ceremonies were held in May 1989.

A panoramic view of the new Comiskey Park. The park was built to enable the Sox to compete financially with the Cubs.

Playing their final season in the old park, the White Sox surprised everyone in 1990. They finished in second place, due mainly to relief pitcher Bobby Thigpen who shattered the major-league mark by recording fifty-seven saves. The next year, the club christened the new Comiskey Park with another second-place finish as first baseman Frank Thomas emerged as one of the game's brightest young sluggers.

With Thomas hitting a franchise-record forty-one homers and Jack McDowell winning twenty-two games and the Cy Young Award, the Sox won the American League West Division title in 1993 under manager Gene Lamont. Their quest for a pennant, however, was thwarted by the Toronto Blue Jays who defeated them in the American League Championship Series (ALCS).

Heavily favored to win the new Central Division title in 1994, the Sox lived up to their promise behind a Most Valuable Player year by Thomas. Unfortunately, a players' strike wiped out the final quarter of the regular season, the play-offs, and the World Series.

Defections due to free agency caused the 1995 team to drop in the standings. It marked the fifth time in franchise history that the club followed up a first-place finish by tumbling into the second division the next season. Despite showing a willingness to spend money to give Chicago a winning team, Reinsdorf could not put an end to the curse.

The start of the new millennium saw the Sox compile the best record in the American League during the regular season. Their ninety-five wins under manager Jerry Manuel in 2000 was their highest total since 1983. However, they could not continue their magic in the play-offs. The Seattle Mariners swept Chicago in three straight games as the major leagues' highest-scoring offense was held to a total of just seven runs.

A New Century

More than eighty years have gone by since the last time a Chicago team (either the White Sox or the Cubs) won a World Series. Those still around who remember the last championship Sox club of Joe Jackson, Eddie Collins, and Ed Cicotte are rare. The years have seen Hall of Famers like Ted Lyons, Luke Appling, and Nellie Fox give their all for the White Sox but come up short in the quest for the elusive ring.

*Jose Valentin slides into third base under the tag of Cleveland Indians
infielder Travis Fryman. Valentin is part of the new generation of White
Sox players that seems capable of breaking the Comiskey Curse.*

The new stars of today, however, like outfielder Magglio Or-
donez, first baseman Paul Konerko, and pitchers Mark Buehrle
and Keith Foulke, give White Sox followers hope for the future.
Together with a new generation of fans, they are ready and willing to put the Comiskey Curse to rest once and for all and to
bring glory back to the Second City.

CHAPTER 2

Joe Jackson

"Shoeless" Joe Jackson is one of baseball's mythic figures. Unfortunately, he is best remembered today as a member of the 1919 Black Sox. Because of his involvement in this scandal, he has been denied a place among baseball's immortals in the Hall of Fame. What cannot be denied is that he was one of the greatest natural hitters the game has ever produced.

A Poor Southern Existence

Joseph Jefferson Wofford Jackson was born in Pickens County, South Carolina, on July 16, 1888. He was the son of former sharecropper George Elmore Jackson and his wife, Martha. Joe's father eventually got a job at a cotton mill in the town of Brandon Mill on the outskirts of the city of Greenville. The job provided him with a regular paycheck that helped put food on the table for the growing family, which included eight children—six boys and two girls.

Since most families in the region had to struggle to make ends meet, children also worked in the mill to bring in extra money. Joe had a job sweeping floors when he was thirteen, but likely began working there when he was even younger. This made school attendance an impossibility. In the little free time he had, Joe played informal games of baseball with the other boys.

Joe was a quiet, gangly youngster who excelled at these games. When he was just thirteen years old, he was asked to play on the Brandon Mill team. He received $2.50 a game for his efforts. (Many small towns in South Carolina were built around their mills and factories. The mills sponsored baseball teams that provided entertainment for the workers and their families.)

Since Joe could throw harder than any of the older players on the team, he began as a pitcher. After he broke a batter's arm with a pitch, however, no one wanted to hit against him. He was switched to the outfield where his talent for hitting, fielding, and throwing soon made him the star of the team and a local celebrity.

When Joe was just fifteen, a local fan named Charlie Ferguson gave him a bat he had made out of hickory. He blackened the thirty-six-inch, forty-eight-ounce piece of wood (much heavier than those used today) with tobacco juice because he knew Joe liked black bats. Joe loved the bat and named it Black Betsy. He eventually took it with him to the major leagues.

A 1910 portrait of "Shoeless" Joe Jackson in a suit and bow tie.

"Shoeless" Joe

Joe played for several mill teams while in his teens and his reputation quickly spread. A former major leaguer named Tom Stouch played against him and came away impressed. "When he hit," said Stouch, "he left a trail of blue flame behind them [the balls] as they shot through the air."[8] When Stouch became the player-manager of the Greenville Spinners of the Class D Carolina Association in 1908, he approached Joe about playing for him. Joe signed for a salary of seventy-five dollars a month, more than twice what he had been making at the mill.

Joe had a lot to learn about the finer points of the game, but he was a natural hitter. He quickly became a fan favorite, stroking line drives to all parts of the field. One day, while playing against the Anderson team, Joe was trying out a new pair of spiked shoes. They had not been broken in, however, and they were giving him painful blisters on his feet. Rather than sit out, he took the shoes off and played in his stocking feet. Late in the game, he stroked a triple. As he slid safely into third base, an Anderson fan yelled out, "You shoeless bastard, you!"[9] The cry was picked up by a local sportswriter, and from that time on, Joe was known as Shoeless Joe Jackson.

The Majors Come Calling

By late summer, several major-league teams had shown interest in Joe, who was leading the league in batting with an average of .346. In August, the Philadelphia Athletics bought him from the Spinners for $900. He made his major-league debut on August 25 against the Cleveland Naps (now called the Indians). He stroked a run-scoring single on the second pitch he saw and made a good impression on manager Connie Mack. "Evidently Jackson is strong in all respects," Mack told the *Evening Telegraph,* "without a weakness, and will make a great player for us."[10]

Unfortunately, Joe's inability to read or write made him a constant target for teammates and opposing players alike. He left the team to return to Greenville because of homesickness. He played only five games for Philadelphia, batting just .130 in twenty-three at bats.

Although Joe did not want to play in Philadelphia again, he agreed to go to spring training with the Athletics in 1909. He realized he could make more money playing baseball than working in the mill, thereby providing the opportunity for a better life for his new wife, parents, and brothers and sisters.

Mack realized his budding young star was still not ready for the big leagues and sent him to Savannah of the Class C South Atlantic League (SAL) for more seasoning. Joe proceeded to tear up the league, batting over .450 in the first month of the season, drawing comparisons to Detroit Tigers' hitting star Ty Cobb. After leading the SAL in batting, Jackson was recalled by Philadelphia at the end of the regular season. He could not get over his distaste for the city, however. He seemed to lose interest in the game and batted just .176 in five games with the Athletics.

Jackson began the 1910 season with New Orleans of the Southern League. When Connie Mack came to the realization that Jackson would never reach his potential with Philadelphia, he traded him to the Cleveland Naps. "I knew our players didn't like Jackson," explained Mack, "but that isn't why I traded him. I also knew Joe had great possibilities as a hitter. But at the same time things were going none too well for [owner] Charlie Somers in Cleveland and I was anxious to do him a good turn in appreciation for the way he had helped us out in Philadelphia in the early days of the league. So I let him have Jackson." [11]

Joe reported to Cleveland after New Orleans's season ended and found the players to be friendlier than those on the Athletics. He responded by batting .387 in twenty games, again showing promise of becoming one of the best hitters in the game.

Super sluggers Ty Cobb (left) and Joe Jackson (right) pose with their bats. Jackson posted a .408 batting average in his 1911 rookie year, setting a rookie record that still stands.

A Star Is Born in Cleveland

Away from Philadelphia, Jackson began to fulfill his potential. By this time, he had grown to a height of six-foot, one-inch tall and weighed 178 pounds. He got off to a fast start and put together arguably the greatest year ever by a rookie. Jackson batted an incredible .408 (second only to Ty Cobb) in 1911, stroked 233 hits (including 45 doubles), scored 126 runs, and had a slugging percentage of .590.

Jackson began his career as a pitcher, but lacked control of his delivery, and was soon moved to the outfield.

Jackson followed up by batting .395 in 1912 and .373 in 1913. In both seasons he again trailed only Cobb. Many, however, considered him to be an even better all-around player than the Georgia Peach (as Cobb was nicknamed). Jackson had a stronger arm and played better defense than his counterpart in Detroit. As Jackson's play improved, so too did that of the Cleveland team. The Naps rose to third place in the American League in 1913 while setting a franchise attendance record.

Cleveland's progress was halted the following year. A new circuit called the Federal League came into existence and began raiding American and National League teams for players. The Naps lost several key performers and dropped into last place. Jackson was hindered by a knee injury and saw his average fall to .338.

That winter, Jackson began to develop an interest in vaudeville. Seeing the theater as a way to supplement his baseball income, he put together a show called "Joe Jackson's Baseball Girls," which gave fans a chance to hear him talk about baseball and ogle a group of beautiful young women. When spring training came around in 1915, he reported out of shape and dropped hints that he might consider quitting baseball to pursue a career on the stage.

Jackson eventually got his mind back on his job and by midseason he was hitting .350. The Naps, however, continued to struggle. With the team in serious financial trouble, owner Charles Somers began to entertain offers for Jackson. On August 20, 1915, he traded his star outfielder to the Chicago White Sox in exchange for three players and $31,500. It was the most expensive deal in baseball history up to that time.

World Champs

While with Cleveland, Jackson had developed a reputation for spending money. He invested in a poolroom in Greenville, bought a house for his parents, bought a large farm for himself, and spent large amounts of cash on clothes and cars. He welcomed the trade to the White Sox, since Chicago was a contender for the pennant. This meant an opportunity to make more money in the World Series.

Jackson continued his outstanding all-around play for Chicago. He batted .341 in 1916 and led the league in triples for the second time. The White Sox finished in second place, two games behind Boston. The next year, nagging injuries hampered his hitting abilities and his average dropped to .301. The White Sox, however, won the pennant, then defeated the New York Giants in six games in the World Series.

All was not well, though, in Chicago. Owner Charles Comiskey was considered one of the cheapest owners in baseball.

Rumors had the White Sox players receiving a $1,500-per-man bonus for their Series victory. In reality, all Comiskey did was send a case of champagne to the players' victory party.

When World War I escalated in 1918, Jackson (who had been classified I-A, meaning he was among those most qualified to be drafted) left the team and took a draft-exempt job at the Bethlehem Steel shipyards. He continued playing ball in the Bethlehem Steel League while receiving criticism from many quarters for avoiding the draft. "There is no room on my club," raged Comiskey, "for players who wish to evade the army draft by entering the employ of shipbuilders."[12] Those feelings, however, did not prevent Comiskey from welcoming Jackson back after Armistice Day.

The 1919 World Series

With Jackson and the rest of the regulars back following the end of the war, the White Sox proceeded to bounce back to the top of the American League standings in 1919, winning the pennant by three and a half games. Jackson batted .351 and finished in the top five in the league in batting, total bases, hits, slugging average, triples, and runs batted in. The Sox entered the World Series as heavy favorites to defeat the Cincinnati Reds for the championship. The Reds, however, stunned the baseball world and won five of the eight games to take the title. Rumors that the Series was fixed made the rounds, but no formal charges were made.

The following year, Jackson put together one of his greatest seasons. He would lead the league in triples for the third time and finish in the top five in batting average (third), slugging average (third), home runs (fifth), total bases (third), runs batted in (fourth), hits (third), and doubles (third). During the course of the season, however, more questions were raised concerning crookedness in baseball. Well-known gambler—and former major leaguer—Billy Maharg suggested that several games during the 1920 season had been fixed by Chicago players, as well as the 1919 Series. That fall, a Cook County grand jury was persuaded to look into the matter. When Jackson and White Sox pitcher Eddie Cicotte were called to testify, the story began to come out.

Cicotte admitted to receiving $10,000 to throw games in the Series. Jackson said he had been told of the fix and was promised

$20,000. According to Jackson, pitcher Lefty Williams came to his hotel room and gave him an envelope with $5,000. Jackson said he did not want the money, but Williams tossed it on the floor and left. Jackson said he tried to tell Charles Comiskey about the money but could not get to see him. He even asked to be benched to avoid any suspicion about being involved in the scheme, but his request was denied. (Comiskey, apparently, was now trying to cover up his own knowledge of the fix.) Jackson contended that he played to win in the Series, pointing to his .375 batting average and twelve hits that set a Series record. He also handled thirty balls in the field without committing an error.

Jackson slides into third base under the instruction of the base coach in a 1915 game.

*Jackson steals second base during the opening game of the crooked 1919
World Series with the Cincinnati Reds. Jackson was banned from
professional baseball for his part in the scandal.*

In a story that may or may not be true, Charlie Owens of the
Chicago Daily News reported that a small boy approached Jackson as he was leaving the grand jury hearings. With tears in his
eyes, the youngster looked at him and said, "Say it ain't so,
Joe." [13] The story has become one of the sport's most famous
tales.

Jackson and seven other players were indicted in the scheme.
By the time they went to trial in July 1921, the transcripts of the
grand jury testimony had mysteriously disappeared. The jury
eventually found all the defendants not guilty on all charges. The

very next day, however, newly appointed baseball commissioner Judge Kenesaw Mountain Landis banned the eight players from ever playing professional baseball again.

Living in Disgrace

Jackson was thirty-three years old and at the height of his career when he was banished by Landis. Together with his wife, Katie, he returned to Greenville where he opened a dry-cleaning business. He later also operated a barbecue restaurant and a liquor store.

However, Jackson found he could not stay away from the game he loved. He began playing semipro ball under the name Joe Joseph in Westwood, New Jersey, in 1922. He could not hide his identity for long, however. The following year, he played for a team in Bastrop, Louisiana, then signed with the Americus, Georgia, club of the South Georgia League.

During this period, Jackson filed a suit against Comiskey for back pay, claiming the three-year contract he signed in 1920 had been illegally terminated. During the course of the proceedings, one of Comiskey's lawyers produced the missing transcripts from the 1921 trial. The embarrassed owner denied having any knowledge of how the papers turned up in his possession, but it seemed obvious that they had been taken to hide Comiskey's early awareness of the scandal. The jury eventually found in Jackson's favor, but the judge overturned the verdict. Since Jackson's testimony contradicted what was in the missing transcripts, it was obvious that he had lied at one of the two trials. (In 1920, Jackson told the grand jury that he agreed to help lose the Series for $20,000, but only recieved $5,000 from Williams after Game Four. In his suit against Comiskey, he said he never agreed to throw the Series, and did not even know about the fix until after the Series was over.) Jackson accepted a small settlement from Comiskey and returned home to South Carolina.

Jackson continued playing semipro ball until he was forty-four years old. In the meantime, his dry-cleaning business prospered. The illiterate ex-ballplayer had become a successful businessman.

Back in the Public Eye

In 1933, Jackson applied to Landis for reinstatement in order to be able to accept a position as player-manager in a new Class D league. Landis denied his request, saying, "The game played in a small town in a Class D league is no less important to the spectators and players than is the game played in the large city in a high class league."[14]

Although professional baseball turned its back on Jackson, the people of Greenville still admired their local hero. He taught the game to neighborhood kids, served as supervisor of umpires for a local league, and coached in the mill leagues.

In June 1939, baseball honored a group of its all-time greats at the dedication of the National Baseball Hall of Fame and Museum in Cooperstown, New York. Joe Jackson was not among the players honored, even though his career batting average was the third highest of all time.

By that time, Jackson was content with his life. He enjoyed being a local celebrity and claimed to have no regrets about any of his actions. "Regardless of what anybody says," he said in a 1942 interview, "I'm innocent of any wrongdoing. I gave baseball all I had. The Supreme Being is the only one to whom I've got to answer."[15]

Jackson's case came before the public eye again in 1951 when he was elected to the Cleveland Hall of Fame in a newspaper poll of fans. The producers of television's *The Ed Sullivan Show* (at that time called *Toast of the Town*) asked him to come to New York for an appearance. In failing health, he accepted the offer. Unfortunately, ten days before his scheduled appearance, on December 5, 1951, Jackson suffered a heart attack and died at the age of sixty-three.

In the years since then, the movement to have Jackson forgiven for his involvement in the scandal has grown. It is widely accepted that his worst offense was knowing of the fix and not reporting it. In 1999, the U.S. House of Representatives passed a resolution calling for him to be honored. As Representative Jim DeMint, author of the bill, said, "It is worthy for this body to take a few minutes to stand up for fairness and right an old wrong."[16]

Many former players have also taken up the cause. As former Boston Red Sox slugger Ted Williams said in 1998, "[Jackson's] served his sentence and it's time for baseball to acknowledge his debt is paid and the Hall of Fame Committee on Veterans to list him as a nominee. It's time, and it's the right thing to do." [17]

Whether or not Joe Jackson should be allowed to join baseball's other immortals in the Hall of Fame is open to question. He is certainly one of the greatest all-around players to ever put on a uniform. Of that there can be no argument.

CHAPTER 3

Nellie Fox

Nellie Fox, the five-foot, nine-inch tall "Mighty Mite" (as he was called by the media), was the heart and soul of the White Sox teams of the 1950s and early 1960s. Despite his size, he rarely missed a game because of injury. He was an accomplished batter and brilliant fielder who played the game with a childish exuberance. Fox was named to the All-Star team twelve times and received baseball's highest accolade when he was elected to the Hall of Fame in 1997.

A Small-Town Existence

Jacob and Mae Fox of St. Thomas, Pennsylvania (a small community of five hundred located approximately 140 miles west of Philadelphia), celebrated Christmas Day 1927 with the birth of their third son, Jacob Nelson, whom they called Nellie. Frank, their firstborn, died when he was just three months old. Wayne, the second son, was born seven years before Nellie.

Jake was a carpenter by trade. He loved baseball and played ball for the St. Thomas town team for more than two decades. He passed up a chance to play pro ball in order to help out on his father's farm. Jake passed on his love for the sport to his sons. According to family lore, the day Nellie was born, Jake went out and bought him his first glove.

Nellie enjoyed all sports and activities, including baseball, soccer, hunting, fishing, and swimming. He demonstrated his competitive nature at an early age, even when playing marbles. As boyhood pal Nip Statler recalled, "I remember that we would draw a circle in the dirt in front of his house and he would end up beating everyone and taking their marbles."[18]

When Nellie was six years old, he became the mascot and batboy for the town team. The club, which included his father, was made up of players from their late teens to mid-thirties. At age ten, he pestered the coach into getting him into a game against the Newville team as a pinch hitter. To the surprise of everyone, as his father later related, he "got a single over second."[19] When Nellie made the team as a regular several years later, it was one of his father's greatest joys to play alongside him.

By the time Nellie was thirteen years old, he was playing on the St. Thomas Vocational High School team, although he was just in the seventh grade. He also played soccer at St. Thomas. "I think I liked soccer better than baseball for a while," he said years later. "I was only about 130 pounds, but I liked the contact. I liked to mix it up."[20]

It was not long before he decided that his future was in baseball. School became less and less important to him. "I had to be a ball player," he said. "I wasn't very good at school and I didn't have any outside hobbies. I played ball. That's what I did. That's what I always wanted to do."[21]

Nelson "Nellie" Fox smiles for a 1950 trading-card photo. Fox was the centerpiece of the White Sox throughout the 1950s and early 1960s.

The Pros Come Calling

In 1944, the Philadelphia Athletics were holding their wartime spring training camp in Frederick, Maryland. Nellie, who had recently turned sixteen, begged his father to take him, and his dad finally agreed. "My idea," explained Jake, "was to keep him in high school. I figured once he had a chance to try out with these big leaguers and saw how good they were, that maybe he'd be willing to wait a while. I figured they'd just tell him to go back to school."[22]

What Jake didn't realize was that many of the country's best players had been called off to military service. Because of that, teams were willing to look at anyone who showed any hint of talent. Philadelphia's legendary manager, Connie Mack, was impressed by the youngster's hustle and work ethic. Years later, Fox's assessment of the situation was more modest. "I don't think I was any ball of fire," he said. "But I was draft-proof for a couple of years, so they decided to keep me."[23]

Mack offered Nellie a minor-league contract, which he accepted. He was assigned to the Lancaster (Pennsylvania) Red Roses of the Class B Inter-State League where he began his professional career as a first baseman.

In twenty-four games with Lancaster, Nellie batted .325 but struggled in the field. It became obvious that his height made him better suited for another position. The Athletics sent him down to their Class D farm team in Jamestown (New York) where the pressure to succeed was not as great. He helped lead the Falcons to the Pony League title by batting .304 while playing the outfield. He also made a great impression on Jamestown owner Harry Bisgeier. "This kid will go on to the majors some day," said Bisgeier, "because he will just naturally fight his way up there."[24]

Nellie returned to Lancaster the following spring. When former star prospect Bill James joined the club, Fox was shifted to second base. He learned the new position quickly and finished the year batting .314 and leading the league in runs scored, hits, and triples.

Fox was promoted to Toronto of the International League in 1946. His journey to the majors was interrupted, however, when he was drafted into the military shortly after turning eighteen. He was discharged in May of the following year and expected to be reassigned to Toronto. Athletics' manager Mack, however, had other plans for him.

A Cup of Coffee with the Athletics

Mack thought highly of young Fox and wanted to expose him to the major-league scene. He ordered him to join the big-league team in Cleveland where the Athletics were playing the Indians. In the second game of a doubleheader on Sunday, June 8, Fox made his major-league debut as a pinch hitter, grounding out against future Hall of Fame pitcher Bob Feller. Nellie appeared in six more games over the next month and a half, going hitless in three at bats. He was sent down to Lancaster and finished the year hitting .281.

Fox fields a ground ball at a 1953 training camp. In his first full season with the Sox, the second baseman was a consistent hitter, striking out only seventeen times in 457 at bats.

In the spring of 1948, Fox was assigned to the Athletics' Lincoln farm team in the Class A Western League. He batted .311 for the year and was named to the league's All-Star team. In September, he was recalled by Philadelphia and appeared in three more games.

The following spring, Fox made the Athletics' opening day roster. Although just twenty-one years of age, he looked older because of the chaw of chewing tobacco he constantly kept in his cheek, a habit he had picked up several years earlier.

When second baseman Pete Suder suffered an injury in June, Fox replaced him in the starting lineup. He batted .255 in fifty-five games that year. On defense, he helped the club set a new American League record for double plays with 217. All in all, Fox did an admirable job as a reserve. That made it all the more shocking to him when he was traded to the White Sox in exchange for catcher Joe Tipton that October. It would turn out to be one of the most lopsided deals in major-league history.

A Brand-New Start

Cass Michaels began the 1950 season as Chicago's second baseman. However, when the Sox quickly fell into last place, he was traded to the Washington Senators on Memorial Day. Fox now had his chance to win the regular job. He did not blow it. His energy and enthusiasm helped spark the team, which rose to sixth place in the standings. Fox finished his first season as a regular with a .247 batting average in 130 games. Although he did not hit for power (no home runs and thirty runs batted in), he consistently made contact with the ball. In 457 at bats, he struck out only seventeen times.

During the off-season, the White Sox began undergoing a transformation. Paul Richards was hired as manager, and numerous players were added through general manager Frank Lane's trades. The moves had a positive effect on the team, adding speed to an offense that desperately needed it. With the club becoming more aggressive on the base paths, people began referring to them as the Go-Go Sox.

To show the city's support for the team, Chicago mayor Martin Kennelly declared May 28 as White Sox Day. Caught up in the spirit, White Sox executive Chuck Comiskey (grandson of Charles) said he thought the Sox had a chance to win the pennant. Explaining his optimism, he said, "I'd say the main [reason] is little Nellie Fox. He's the sparkplug. While everybody deserves credit for making us one of the most spirited teams in baseball, it wasn't until Fox caught fire that we really exploded."[25]

To the surprise of many, the White Sox were in first place by mid-June and Fox was leading the league in batting with a .364 average. That July, he made the All-Star team for the first of twelve times. However, both Fox and the Sox saw their performances drop off in the second half of the season. Chicago eventually finished in fourth place. Their 81–73 record was an improvement of twenty-one games over their mark of the previous year. For his part, Fox finished with a .313 batting average (fifth in the American League) and 189 hits (second in the circuit). Nellie gave much of the credit for his improvement at the plate to Chicago coach Roger "Doc" Cramer. As Howard Roberts of the *Chicago Daily News* service reported, "Cramer taught him how to bunt, broke him of the bad habit of hitting off his front foot, and persuaded him to use a heavier bat with a larger barrel."[26]

The fans appreciated the team's improved performance. The Sox showed a home attendance of over 1 million for the first time in franchise history. Paul Richards credited Fox with more than just inspiring the team in the field. "Fox, perhaps more than any other individual, saved the Chicago American League franchise for the Comiskey family," said Richards. "When I was brought in to manage the club, a bank was getting ready to take over. He restored the White Sox to respectability."[27]

The Mighty Mite

Over the next several years, Fox established himself as one of the top second basemen in the game. Through the rest of the decade, his batting average slipped below .290 just one time (.285 in 1953). Using his trademark bottle bat, he led the league in hits four times and in singles a record-setting eight times. He rarely struck out, never fanning more than eighteen times in a season.

In the field, Fox was a magician with the glove. He won three Gold Glove Awards for fielding supremacy, and won the

Fox fouls the ball down the first base line in a 1955 game against the New York Yankees. In the 1955 season Fox began an impressive streak of 798 consecutive games played.

defensive Triple Crown three times (leading American League second basemen in fielding percentage, putouts, and assists in 1952, 1956, and 1959).

Fox rarely missed a game, playing through cuts, bruises, illnesses, and fatigue. He had played in 255 consecutive games when White Sox manager Marty Marion sat him out to give him a rest on August 6, 1955. When he returned to the lineup two days later, he began a streak of 798 straight games played—a record for second basemen. The fact that he performed this "iron man" feat at his diminutive size made the mark all the more impressive and helped earn him the nickname of the "Mighty Mite."

1959 American League Champs

By the time the 1959 season began, Fox was recognized by most observers as the best all-around second baseman in the American

League. Al Lopez, the White Sox manager, referred to him as "what you call a 'manager's ball player.' He does his job expertly and he does it every day. He's the type of player you can count on. He's an 'old pro.' A great many times, he is hurting pretty badly from the dumpings he has taken on the field, but he's always ready to play. Fox is a self-made ball player. He has hustled his way to stardom."[28]

Fox set the tone for the White Sox's 1959 season on opening day. The Sox met the Detroit Tigers at Briggs Stadium on April 10. Fox had five hits in the contest including a two-run homer in the fourteenth inning to win the game for Chicago. This helped the team get off to a quick start while the perennial American League champion New York Yankees, besieged by injuries, dropped to the bottom of the standings. Fox and Aparicio led the team at bat, in the field, and on the base paths. By June, Chicago had established itself as a bona fide pennant contender. They did so using an offense that depended more on speed than on power. In recognition of their roles in helping the team to its position in the standings, both Fox and Aparicio were named as starters in the All-Star Games. (To generate income for the players' pension fund, two games were played each year from 1959 to 1962.)

The second half of the season turned into a race between the White Sox and the Cleveland Indians. Chicago improved its chances when it acquired slugging first baseman Ted Kluszewski from the Pittsburgh Pirates in August. Four days before, on August 21, the White Sox did something they had never before done in the club's long history: They honored one of their players with a "night." The player so honored was the Mighty Mite, Nellie Fox. As Dick Hackenberg of the *Sun-Times* wrote, "They're holding a 'night' for Nellie Fox at Comiskey Park Friday. Nellie doesn't need a night—not like the White Sox and Chicago need Nellie. . . . This is no charity event. This is the expression of a city's appreciation for the hustlingest ball player in the business."[29]

In the game following the ceremonies, Aparicio and Fox demonstrated the manner in which they sparked the Chicago offense. In the very first inning, Aparicio singled and Fox was hit by a pitch. The pair then pulled off a double steal, and when the catcher's throw went into left field, Aparicio scored. Chicago held on to record a one-run victory over Washington.

The White Sox went on to win the pennant by five games. Fox's contributions to the team's success were recognized by the baseball writers when they voted him the American League's Most Valuable Player. (Aparicio finished second in the voting and Sox pitcher Early Wynn came in third.) In one of his best all-around seasons, Fox finished first in the league in games played (156) and at bats (624), second in hits (191) and doubles (34), fourth in batting (.306), and seventh in on-base percentage (.380)

Fox poses with fellow infielder Luis Aparicio (left) in a 1959 photograph. The pair proved pivotal to the success of the team that season, as the Sox overtook the Cleveland Indians for the American League pennant.

and triples (6). In the field, he committed just ten errors to win his second Gold Glove Award.

In the Series that fall, the White Sox fell to the Los Angeles Dodgers in six games despite Fox's brilliant play. At the plate, he batted .375 with nine hits including three doubles. He also handled thirty-seven chances flawlessly in the field. The Dodgers were better, however, and the Sox had to be satisfied with their first pennant in forty years.

On to Houston

The 1959 season was the last in which Fox reached the .300 mark in batting. As he approached his mid-thirties, his production began to decline. His averages over the next four seasons were .289, .251, .267, and .260. Over that same span, the White Sox never got within ten games of first place.

Fox surpassed the 2,500-hit mark in July 1963, but his days with the White Sox were numbered. Two months after the end of the season, he was traded to the National League Houston Colt .45s where his former manager Paul Richards was general manager. Fox's departure was a shock to White Sox fans everywhere and signified the end of the Go-Go Sox.

In Houston, Fox joined a young team beginning its third year of existence. The Colt .45s (now the Astros) entered the National League in 1962 along with the New York Mets. Fox's value to the club lay as much in his ability to serve as a teacher and example for the team's young players, like Joe Morgan and Sonny Jackson, as for his ability to still perform on the field. As manager Harry Craft explained, "Nellie always has been an aggressive, intelligent and inspirational player. He should prove to be a model to our youngsters."[30]

Fox batted .265 in his one full season with Houston. At age thirty-six, he was given his release as a player, then signed with Houston as a coach. In 1965, he was activated in May when Morgan slumped, but he appeared in only twenty-one games. By the time he finally hung up his spikes, he had amassed 2,663 hits in nineteen major-league seasons.

The Road to the Hall of Fame

Fox remained with Houston as a coach through the 1967 season. He then became first base coach and hitting instructor for the

Puffing on a corncob pipe, Fox watches the action of a 1957 game from the comfort of the dugout.

Washington Senators under manager Ted Williams. When he finally left the game in 1972, he returned to Pennsylvania where he operated a bowling alley. Tragically, he was diagnosed with cancer shortly afterward. Fox died on December 1, 1975, just shy of his forty-eighth birthday.

Fox became eligible for the Hall of Fame in 1971, but in fifteen years on the ballot, he never received enough votes from the baseball writers to win election. In his final year of eligibility, he missed selection by just two ballots, the closest losing margin in the history of the voting. He finally gained admittance when he was named by the Veterans Committee in 1997. It was only fitting that his election came after a long battle. As Tom Withers of the Associated Press wrote that day, "Pitchers couldn't strike out Fox and neither could the Hall of Fame."[31]

CHAPTER 4

Minnie Minoso

The first black to wear a White Sox uniform, "Minnie" Minoso was one of the team's most exciting players ever. Chicago owner Jerry Reinsdorf called him Mr. White Sox because he symbolized the spirit of the team better than any other player. A consistent .300 hitter throughout his career, Minoso's speed on the base paths inspired the famous "Go-Go" chant of the 1950s. As former White Sox owner Bill Veeck once said, "I don't believe there is a player in the game today who can give you the thrill he can. Without him in the lineup, it's just another ballgame."[32]

The Sugar Fields of Cuba

Saturnino Orestes Arrieta Armas Minoso was born in El Perico, Cuba, a little more than a hundred miles outside of Havana, on November 29, 1925. (According to official sources he was born in 1922. In his official biography, however, Minoso says he lied when obtaining his visa in order to qualify for the Cuban army.) Orestes was the son of Carlos Arrieta and Cecilia Armas. His mother had four children—two boys and two girls—from a previous marriage to a man named Julian Minoso. Orestes would tag along with brothers Cirilo and Francisco when they played ball for the

Orestes "Minnie" Minoso poses for a 1955 publicity shot. Minoso was the first black player to wear a White Sox uniform.

local factory team. According to Minoso's book, when people saw the three boys, they would call out, "Those are the Minoso brothers and that's little Minoso. He's one of the Minoso brothers."[33] From that time on, he was known as Orestes Minoso.

Orestes's father worked in the sugar fields, as did most of the men in El Perico. His family was poor, as were the families of the other ranch workers, but the young Orestes never felt cheated, since there was always a great deal of love shown. Unfortunately, his parents separated when he was still a young boy and his father moved to Camagüey where there was more work. Orestes moved to Havana with his mother, but she passed away suddenly when he was ten years old. Over the next few years, he lived at various times with his brother, his sister, and his aunt.

Baseball was extremely popular in Cuba, and Orestes took to the game at an early age. He played sandlot ball and also organized a team on the ranch. He was a pitcher with a blazing fastball, far more advanced than the other boys. At the age of twelve, he decided he was going to be a professional ballplayer in the Negro Leagues in the United States when he got older.

The Cuban League

When Orestes moved to Havana as a teenager, he began playing semipro ball, first for the Partagas Cigar Factory team, then for the Ambrosia Candy Factory squad. He was paid two dollars per game and eight dollars a week for working part-time with the company. He began playing third base where his powerful arm was especially valuable.

It was with Ambrosia that Orestes got a piece of advice that served him well the rest of his career. Just before going to bat against a particularly tough veteran pitcher, his manager took him aside and said, "Whatever you do, don't go down with your bat on your shoulder. If the pitch looks hitable, just swing!"[34] Orestes took the advice to heart. From that point on, he always went to the plate with an aggressive attitude.

At age seventeen, in his second year with Ambrosia, Orestes batted .367 to lead the league in hitting. He left the team in 1943 to play with the Cuban Miners, one of the best semipro clubs in all of Cuba. In November of the next year, he got an even bigger opportunity. He was offered a chance to play with the Marianao Tigers of the top league in the country, the Cuban Professional League.

Orestes got off to a quick start with the Tigers, driving home the winning runs in each of his first two games. Shortly after, he was approached by a wealthy Mexican businessman named Jorge Pasquel. Together with his brother, Pasquel had formed a new Mexican League. They had been offering huge amounts of money to many major leaguers in the United States to get them to jump to their new league. Pasquel took out a bag filled with assorted bills and offered Orestes $30,000 to play two seasons in Mexico. It was more money than he had ever seen in his life. Surprisingly, the young Cuban refused. Orestes took fifty dollars out of his pocket and said, "My $50 is like two pennies compared with what you just showed me. But money isn't everything to me. I'm going to America some day."[35]

At the time, there was an unwritten rule that prevented blacks from playing professional baseball in the United States. Pasquel tried to tell Orestes that a black player would be treated like a dog. Still, Orestes would not sign. His dream was to play in the Negro Leagues in America, and he could not be convinced otherwise.

Minoso remained with the Tigers and proceeded to hit .301 to win the league's Rookie of the Year Award. At the end of the season, he got what he was hoping for. Jose Fernandez, one of the coaches at Marianao, was the manager of the New York Cubans team in the Negro League. Fernandez told Cubans' owner Alex Pompez about Minoso. Pompez, in turn, offered Minoso a chance to play with the Cubans. His dream was about to come true.

The Climb to the Majors

When Minoso began playing with the Cubans, he earned $300 a month. More important to him than the money was the chance to come to the United States, a place he had been dreaming about since he was a young boy.

Minoso played with the Cubans for three and a half seasons, improving at the plate each year. Although not a slugger, he had extra base power and excellent speed. Following the All-Star Game in 1948, he was approached by a scout from the Cleveland Indians. The color barrier in the major leagues had been broken the previous year by Jackie Robinson of the Brooklyn Dodgers. The Indians were one of the teams most eager to sign black players. Cleveland scout Bill Killefer had touted Minoso to owner Bill Veeck as the "fastest thing on legs."[36] The Indians purchased his contract from the Cubans and assigned him to their Class A farm team in Dayton, Ohio.

The Indians considered starting Minoso at the major-league level, but the team was in the midst of a pennant race and he would be limited to bench duty. (Cleveland would win the pennant in a play-off with the Red Sox, and defeat the Boston Braves in the World Series.) Instead, at Dayton, he made a good impression by batting .525 in eleven games over the last month of the season. He broke the color barrier with the team and did not let the occasional harassment from other players interfere with his job performance.

The next year, Minoso made the big-league club right out of training camp. He made his major-league debut on April 19 and appeared in seven games before being sent down to San Diego in the Pacific Coast League for more seasoning and to learn the fine points of playing the outfield. Minoso batted .297 with 22 home runs and 75 runs batted in that year. In 1950, he finished second in the league in batting with a .339 mark, stroked 203 hits, and drove in 115 runs.

After another solid spring in 1951, Minoso began the season with the Indians. By late April, he was batting over .400 and getting more and more playing time. Following a doubleheader against the St. Louis Browns in which he got seven hits in eight at bats, he received news that would shake up his life. "Minoso," said manager Al Lopez, "you have just been traded to the Chicago White Sox."[37]

Blazing a Trail in Chicago

Minoso was depressed about leaving Cleveland and somewhat concerned about being the first black to play for the White Sox. However, he was glad to get the chance to play regularly with manager Paul Richards's squad. His debut was a memorable one. Playing the New York Yankees on May 1, 1951, he stepped up to the plate in the first inning to face Vic Raschi. Raschi was a hard-throwing right-hander who had won twenty-one games in each of the previous two seasons (and would do so again in 1951). Batting with one man on and one out, Minoso took the first pitch for a ball, then blasted the next pitch over the center field fence for a two-run home run. The crowd cheered wildly for their new hero.

Minoso went on to bat .326 for the year (second in the league to Ferris Fain), scored 112 runs (second to Dom DiMaggio), and led the American League in stolen bases with 31 and triples with 14. He made the All-Star team for the first time but, surprisingly, finished behind New York's Gil McDougald in the voting by the

baseball writers for the American League Rookie of the Year
Award. (Illogically, in the voting for Most Valuable Player by
those same writers, Minoso finished fourth while McDougald
came in ninth.)

With Minoso's speed added to that of Jim Busby, Jim Rivera,
Chico Carrasquel, and Nellie Fox, the club became known as the
Go-Go Sox. The team led the league in hits, triples, and stolen
bases as it finished in fourth place. Nineteen fifty-one was also

---

Minoso demonstrates his powerful swing. Minoso batted .326 his first year
with the Sox, and went on to bat over .300 four times over six seasons.

Minoso, with his foot on first base, looks poised to lead off and steal second. His speed helped the team lead the league in stolen bases in the 1951 season.

the year that Minoso received his nickname of "Minnie" from a Chicago dentist named Dr. Robinson. (The doctor reportedly was calling for his nurse, named Minnie, and Minoso thought he was referring to him.) Minoso would eventually adopt the name legally.

Perennial Runners-Up

Over the next six seasons, Minoso was the most exciting player on the White Sox team. He batted better than .300 four times from his number three spot in the batting order. His best year, arguably, was 1954. That season, he reached career highs in runs scored (119), runs batted in (116), triples (a league-leading 18), and slugging average (.535).

In addition to being a consistent hitter, Minoso also used other means for getting on base. Because of the way he crowded the plate when batting, he was often hit by pitches. He led the league with a major-league-record six consecutive seasons in that category (1956–1961). Once on base, he used his speed to great advantage, leading the league in stolen bases in each of his first three full years (1951–1953).

Despite getting hit so often, Minoso rarely missed a game. He played ten games with a broken bone in his foot during one stretch. The only time he missed any appreciable time on the field was when he was hit in the head by a pitch from New York's Bob Grim in 1955. He suffered a hairline fracture of the skull but still returned to action in just over two weeks.

Regardless of Minoso's play, the White Sox always fell short of winning the pennant. Chicago won between eighty-one and ninety-four games each year, but could not get past the Yankees and Indians. The Sox finished third five consecutive times (1952–1956) before finally moving up to second in 1957. Chicago led the American League by six games in early June that year before finally settling back behind New York.

Minoso made the All-Star team again in 1957 and drove home the game-winning run in the ninth inning of the midseason contest. In the bottom half of the inning, he threw out a runner at third base and made a great catch on a line drive by Gil Hodges to end the game. Nineteen fifty-seven was also the first year that the Gold Glove Awards were handed out. Minoso was one of the three outfielders to be named, along with future Hall of Famers Willie Mays and Al Kaline.

Despite having a successful season on the field, however, the year ended for Minoso on a sad note.

Moving On

On December 4, 1957, Minoso picked up a newspaper and found out that he had been traded to the Cleveland Indians. The trade was made, in part, to open up room on the Chicago roster for a pair of highly regarded outfield prospects, Johnny Callison and Jim Landis. "I feel like the whole world was over for me," he said. "Like my city . . . had put me out. Like when you leave a place where you were born and raised. You feel funny. I never believed it, that I was traded. But it was true."[38]

Minoso had two successful seasons in Cleveland, batting .302 in both 1958 and 1959. The Indians finished in fourth place in his first season with the Tribe, then rose to second the next year. The team that won the pennant in 1959 was none other than the White

Sox. That December, White Sox owner Bill Veeck (who had taken over the club in 1959) reacquired Minoso. In a thoughtful gesture, he presented him with an honorary championship ring, even though Minnie had not been part of the pennant winning team.

The year 1959 was significant for another reason. It was the year Fidel Castro overthrew the government of Cuban dictator Fulgencio Batista and brought sweeping changes to Minoso's homeland. When Minoso became upset with the Communist regime, he decided to leave the country permanently (he had returned every off season to play winter ball), even though most of his family remained behind. He lost many of his possessions and never returned to his native land.

Yankees catcher Yogi Berra tags Minoso as he slides into home plate in a 1959 game.

Cuban-born Minoso enjoys a winter ball game in Havana with Cuban Prime Minister Fidel Castro. Minoso quickly grew disillusioned with communism and left Cuba for good in 1960.

Back in the States, Minoso responded with another solid season in 1960, leading the American League in hits with 184, batting .311, and driving home 105 runs. After one more year with Chicago, new owner Arthur Allyn Jr. sent him to the St. Louis Cardinals as part of a housecleaning that saw Allyn get rid of several veteran players in an effort to cut salaries.

Injuries, however, limited his effectiveness with St. Louis. With his best days behind him, Minoso moved on to the Washington Senators in 1963, then back to the White Sox for thirty games in 1964. His long major-league career finally seemed to have reached its end.

The Six-Decade Man

Following his release from the White Sox, Minoso got a job doing public relations work for S&H Green Stamps, a company that rewarded consumer purchases with little green stamps that could be redeemed for a variety of goods. He continued to play winter ball in the Mexican League and eventually became a player-manager there. When Bill Veeck took over as White Sox owner for a second time in December 1975, he asked Minoso to return to the club as its first base coach. Minnie quickly accepted.

On September 11, 1976, Veeck reactivated Minoso so that he could become a rare four-decade major-league player. Minnie was nervous about how the fans would receive him. "It's been many years since I face pitching like this," he said. "I hope [the fans] forgive me."[39] Minoso got one hit in eight at bats in three games, becoming the oldest player in history to hit safely in a major-league game.

Four years later, Minoso joined the ranks of active players once again. In September 1980, he was activated for the final three games of the season. He went hitless in two times up as a pinch hitter (fouling out to the catcher both times) to join Nick Altrock as the sport's only five-decade players.

More than a decade later, Minoso made history one more time. On June 30, 1993, he appeared as a designated hitter for the St. Paul Saints in a game against the Thunder Bay Whiskey Jacks of the independent Northern League. After taking two high pitches for balls, Minoso swung at the next pitch from nineteen-year-old Yoshi Seo and hit a hard ground ball to the mound. At age sixty-eight, Minoso had now appeared in professional games in an amazing six consecutive decades.

Minoso's long journey as a player was finally over. In seventeen big-league seasons, he had a lifetime batting average of .298 with 186 home runs and 1,023 runs batted in. He appeared in seven All-Star Games, and won three Gold Gloves for his fielding. Even more important than the numbers, however, was his role as the first Latin American star to make the grade in the major leagues. Since his retirement, Minoso has acted as a baseball ambassador by serving as a community relations representative with the White Sox. Fighting racial prejudice and a language barrier, he has been an inspiration to players of all races and nationalities.

CHAPTER 5

Bill Veeck

B ill Veeck was the consummate baseball showman. His passion for baseball and skills at promotion helped make him the hero of the everyday fan. As an owner, he was dedicated to making the fans' experience at the ballpark an enjoyable one and toward this end introduced, among other things, names on the backs of uniforms and the exploding scoreboard. He will always be remembered, however, as the man who sent up a midget to bat in a big-league game.

Every Young Boy's Dream

William Louis Veeck Jr. was destined for a life in baseball. He was born to William Louis and Grace Veeck on February 9, 1914, in Chicago, Illinois. His father was a sportswriter for the *Chicago Evening American*. When Bill was just three years old, his father wrote a series of articles—under the pen name Bill Bailey—criticizing the Chicago Cubs. Cubs' owner William Wrigley invited Veeck to his home for dinner and in the course of the evening said to him, "All right, if you're so smart why don't you come and do it?" [40] Veeck accepted Wrigley's offer and became vice president and treasurer of the team in 1918. He was named president the following year.

Bill Jr. and his sister were raised in the Chicago suburb of Hinsdale where he attended public school. As the son of the man who ran the ball club, his childhood was every young boy's dream. From an early age, he hung out at the ballpark and got to know the players. When he was old enough, he sold peanuts

A young Bill Veeck pays close attention as Joe McCarthy, manager of the Chicago Cubs, demonstrates how to properly grip the bat.

and scorecards. As he often liked to say, "I'm the only human being ever raised at a ballpark."[41]

After grammar school, Bill attended the prestigious Phillips Academy in Andover, Massachusetts. When he became homesick, he returned to Hinsdale High School for two years. From there he went to the exclusive Los Alamos Ranch School in New Mexico. He did not fit in with his snobbish classmates, however, and became known as "that public school rowdy."[42]

Although he never graduated high school, Bill attended Kenyon College in Ohio where he played football. It was while at Kenyon in 1933 that he received word that his father had died. He left school and returned home to take a job as an office boy with the Cubs for eighteen dollars a week. He continued his education by taking night courses in business, accounting, and engineering at Northwestern University. During his eight years with the team, Bill handled almost every conceivable job, from working the switchboards to helping out with the grounds crew to running the commissary. In 1940, he became the team's treasurer and assistant secretary. It was during this time that Bill came up with the idea of planting ivy on the outfield walls at Wrigley Field. He had no plans, however, to make baseball his career.

When Veeck was twenty-seven, he teamed up with former Cub Charlie Grimm and bought the Milwaukee Brewers, the American Association minor-league farm team of the Cubs. It was at Milwaukee that he began to show his talents as a promoter. Veeck made every day at the ballpark an adventure, with live music and giveaways part of every game. He sat in the stands with the fans, enjoying the games and sharing stories. His son Mike once said of this habit, "I think people look at it as quaint, Dad sitting in the stands. It was just his way of doing market research."[43]

One of the things he found was that many people could not attend night games because of their jobs. To remedy the situation, he started some games at 8:30 A.M., offering free breakfast to those who showed up. The gimmick gained him national attention and helped improve the Brewers' financial picture. Within two years' time, attendance more than tripled.

Back to the Majors

Veeck's baseball sojourn was interrupted by three years of military service with the marines. During his time in the South Pacific, he suffered an injury that would eventually require the amputation of his right leg below the knee. When he returned home, he sold the Brewers for a healthy profit. He turned his attention to finding a major-league team that was for sale. (He had tried to buy the Philadelphia Phillies in 1943 and stock the team with black stars. Commissioner Landis allegedly prevented him from carrying out his plan. This was four years before Jackie Robinson broke baseball's color barrier with the Brooklyn Dodgers.)

In 1946, at the age of thirty-two, Veeck headed a ten-man group that purchased the Cleveland Indians of the American League. The sixth-place Indians had not won a pennant since 1920. Veeck put some of his ideas into effect and became an instant hit. Among his more practical moves were giving away the rights to broadcast Indians games in order to get them on radio, and permanently moving the team from decaying League Park into larger Municipal Stadium. In one of his more inspired promotions, the team held a night for Joe Earley, a fan who complained that the team honored everyone except the average Joe.

Veeck once said, "Baseball by itself is not enough. It's got to be fun even when the home club loses. It's got to be wrapped up like a Christmas package."[44] He also knew, however, that fans would stop coming out if the club did not show improvement. To strengthen the product on the field, Veeck signed the American League's first black player, Larry Doby, in 1947. The next year, he signed Negro League pitching legend Satchel Paige. Many considered this move nothing more than a publicity stunt, but the forty-two-year-old Paige won six of seven decisions in his rookie season.

Veeck's moves quickly bore fruit. In 1946, the Indians drew more than 1 million fans for the first time in their history. The team climbed to fourth place in 1947, then won the pennant the next year in a one-game play-off with the Boston Red Sox. Cleveland set four attendance records during the season, drawing more than 2.25 million fans. In the World Series against the Boston Braves, another mark was set when 86,268 fans came out to see Game 5. The Indians defeated Boston in the six-game Series to win their first championship in twenty-eight years.

The Master Showman

In 1949, Veeck sold the Indians to a local syndicate for $2.2 million. He made the move partly because he needed a new challenge, but mainly because he was forced to liquidate his assets due to divorce proceedings begun by his wife, whom he had married in 1935. He found the ultimate challenge less than two years later when he bought the St. Louis Browns.

The Browns were arguably the worst team in major-league baseball. They had won only one pennant in the franchise's long history, and aside from the war years (when the league was populated by rookies, retreads, and those rejected for military service) had not put together a winning season since 1929.

With St. Louis, Veeck was not able to repeat the success he had with Cleveland. He did, however, stage some of the most memo-

As ball-club owner, Veeck employed showman tactics to draw huge crowds. His most famous stunt occurred in 1951 when he sent midget Eddie Gaedel (pictured) to the plate. Gaedel walked on four pitches.

Jay Edson of the St. Louis Browns solicits help from the fans during Grandstand Managers' Day. Veeck devised the successful promotion to allow fans to vote on managerial decisions for a day.

rable promotions the game of baseball has ever seen. Veeck's most famous stunt occurred on August 19, 1951. That night he sent up three-foot, seven-inch midget Eddie Gaedel as a pinch hitter in the second game of a doubleheader against the Detroit Tigers. When home plate umpire Ed Hurley questioned the move, St. Louis manager Zack Taylor came out to show him Gaedel's contract. Wearing uniform number 1/8, the midget took four pitches for balls and went to first base on a walk. The move brought a moment of delight to the fans who were in attendance, but was not appreciated by American League president Will Harridge. Two days later, Gaedel was barred from appearing in any more games.

Less than a week later, Veeck made headlines again by staging Grandstand Managers' Day. Fans seated in a special section behind the Browns' dugout were given signs with the word YES printed on one side and NO on the other. Every time a situation arose calling for a decision to be made (Shall we warm up a pitcher? Play the infield back?), the votes were counted and the results relayed to the St. Louis dugout. Zack Taylor, the Browns' manager, was given a pair of slippers, a pipe, and a rocking chair in which to sit while the fans made the calls. The promotion was a rousing success as the Browns scored a 5–3 win to end a four-game losing streak.

Between Teams

Although the Browns' attendance more than doubled in 1952, the team still remained at the bottom of the league standings. Veeck attempted to relocate the club to Baltimore, but was denied permission by the other American League owners (who had become less than enamored with him because of his stunts). Veeck eventually won their approval to move, but only on the condition that he sell the team. The Browns were sold to a syndicate headed by Baltimore mayor Tom D'Alesandro and moved to Baltimore for the 1954 season.

Over the next six years, Veeck tried unsuccessfully to buy the Philadelphia Athletics and Detroit Tigers baseball teams, as well as the Ringling Brothers–Barnum and Bailey Circus. He opened a public relations firm in Cleveland, did commentary on television, bought a ranch in New Mexico, became a sectional scout for the Indians, and ran the Miami minor-league franchise in the International League.

Finally, in March 1959, Veeck's efforts to buy another major-league team met with success. His syndicate purchased 54 percent ownership in the Chicago White Sox from Dorothy Comiskey Rigney, granddaughter of Charles Comiskey.

Another Pennant

Veeck took over a team that was poised to make a serious run at the American League pennant. The key players were already in place, but Veeck did not think the team had enough hitting to win. To his surprise, the White Sox played up to their potential and proved him wrong by winning their first flag since 1920. In his defense, he later explained, "There's always two ways to approach something like that. You could say, 'We're gonna win the pennant.' And you don't. Then everyone's disappointed. If you start by saying, 'We should win this thing,' you haven't achieved anything, really. All you've done is added a burden to playing. So I would rather be wrong that way."[45]

Veeck helped develop a winning attitude among both the players and fans. He ran a string of promotions that included cow-milking contests, Martians landing on the infield at Comiskey Park (featuring former St. Louis Brown Eddie Gaedel as one of the tiny aliens), and numerous giveaways.

The following season, his belief that the team needed more hitting resulted in a series of trades in which several young prospects were surrendered. "I could've made them another way, but in any event, we were going to go for broke. I wasn't interested in what was gonna happen five years down the road. I wanted to win back-to-back." [46] Unfortunately, such was not to be the case. The Sox finished the year in third place, ten games off

Veeck smiles as he completes paperwork. As owner of the White Sox, Veeck did little to direct the team to a winning season, but he did run a number of popular promotions.

the pace. The season was a success financially, however, with a record 1,644,460 fans passing through the gates, many to see the Sox's new $350,000 exploding scoreboard that erupted when Chicago players hit a home run, and the fireworks displays that followed the games. Veeck also made it easier to follow the players by having the White Sox become the first team to wear uniforms with the players' names on the backs.

The aging Sox dropped to fourth place in 1961, but Veeck was not around to see it. Suffering from a reduced blood flow to the brain and a chronic cough, he was advised by his physicians to sell the team. "The doctors tell me that I'm likely to be out of action for six or seven months," he said, "and I know you can't run a ball club in absentia."[47] On June 12, he sold his interest in the team to Arthur Allyn Jr.

Chicago White Sox, Act 2

During his recuperation, Veeck wrote his autobiography. He also ran Suffolk Downs racetrack for three years, all the while plotting his return to baseball. He finally got his chance in 1975. In December of that year, Veeck headed a group that bought 80 percent of the White Sox from John Allyn (Arthur's brother). White Sox fans—having heard rumors that the team would move to Seattle—welcomed him back with open arms.

Shortly after he took over, however, the rules of the game changed dramatically. The reserve clause was voided when federal arbitrator Peter Seitz declared pitchers Andy Messersmith and Dave McNally free agents. (Up to then, the reserve clause bound a player for life to the team that originally signed him.) Unable to spend money like the wealthier clubs, the White Sox fell to last place in 1976, twenty-five and a half games out of first.

Veeck decided a change in strategy was needed if the Sox were to compete. He developed what became known as a "rent-a-player" scheme whereby he obtained players in the last year of their contract, knowing full well he would not be able to re-sign them. He traded for outfielders Richie Zisk and Oscar Gamble, and the duo helped rejuvenate the team's offense. Between them, they slugged 61 homers and drove in 184 runs in 1977 for a team that had been transformed into the "South Side Hit Men." Veeck also signed several second-tier free agents, players who were either coming back from injuries or were too old to warrant more lucrative deals.

The Sox improved by twenty-five and a half games in 1977, finished a surprising third in the American League West, and set a franchise attendance record. As Veeck would later say, "I have never seen anywhere the kind of enthusiasm that was engendered in this ballpark in '77."[48] He received much credit for the team's resurgence and was named the United Press International (UPI) Executive of the Year.

Unfortunately, Veeck could not continue to perform his magic. The Sox dropped to fifth place in 1978 and remained there the following two seasons. The team still drew fairly well at the gate, however, as Veeck's innovations and promotions continued to garner national attention. On August 8, 1976, he had the Sox take the field in shorts rather than their regular uniform pants. He also put a public address microphone in the broadcast booth so announcer Harry Caray could lead the crowd in a rendition of "Take Me Out to the Ball Game" during the seventh-inning stretch. One promotion, however, turned out to be a complete disaster.

Disco Demolition Night

Trying to capitalize on the antidisco sentiment that was rampant that summer, the Sox announced they would hold Disco Demolition Night on July 12, 1979. Any fan who came to Comiskey Park with a disco record would be allowed in for just ninety-eight cents. In between games of the doubleheader against the Tigers, the records would be placed in a Dumpster on the field and destroyed.

The Sox, however, underestimated just how many people hated disco. More than fifty thousand fans got into the game, while another fifteen thousand milled around outside the stadium, a large portion of them already drunk. During the first game, records flew out of the stands onto the field while firecrackers went off near the visiting team's dugout. When the records were destroyed between games, the crowd went crazy. Thousands of fans ran onto the field, tearing up the mound, starting a bonfire in center field, and tearing down sections of the bull pen fence. Riot police were called in to restore order, but the Sox

Veeck organized his most outrageous promotion, Disco Demolition Night, on July 12, 1979. The event turned ugly when thousands of fans ran amok on the field and riot police were called in to restore order.

were forced to forfeit the second game. "The promotion was too good," recalled Veeck. "It was a disaster only because if we had had any idea what was going to happen, we could've controlled it. But it had never occurred to anybody. They kept coming and coming and coming."[49]

The End of the Line

The difficulties trying to field a competitive team with limited resources finally got to Veeck in 1980. The Sox could not afford the salaries paid to second-level players, let alone the stars. ("I don't mind the high price of stardom," said the owner. "I just don't like the high price of mediocrity."[50]) Veeck began shopping the team around, finally selling to real estate mogul Jerry Reinsdorf for $19 million in January 1981.

Following his retirement from the game, Veeck spent much of his free time at Cubs games, sitting shirtless in the bleachers at Wrigley Field and talking with the fans. (Never one for formal dress, Veeck always went tieless because of a chronic skin condition that made tight collars unbearable.)

Veeck fought health problems throughout his life, and underwent two operations for lung cancer in 1984. He finally passed away on January 2, 1986. The funeral services were held at the Church of St. Thomas the Apostle in Chicago. It was only fitting that a lone trumpeter opened the services playing Aaron Copland's *Fanfare for the Common Man.* Veeck's entire career was spent fighting the establishment to make the game more enjoyable for the everyday fan on the street.

CHAPTER 6

Dick Allen

Although Dick Allen played just two and a half seasons with Chicago, former White Sox general manager Roland Hemond credited him with being the "savior of the franchise." His displays of power hitting helped bring about a renewed interest in White Sox baseball. Allen is the only Chicago player ever to lead the American League in runs batted in, and one of only two to lead in home runs. Unfortunately, he also led the league in controversy, constantly feuding with teammates, managers, writers, and fans.

"Sleepy" Allen from Wampum, Pennsylvania

Richard Anthony Allen was born on March 8, 1942, in tiny Wampum, Pennsylvania, approximately thirty miles northwest of Pittsburgh. The Allen family—consisting of his mother and father, four brothers, and four sisters—was the only black family in the area. Dick's dad had his own trash-hauling business. Era, his mother, was part Cherokee Indian. When his parents separated, the job of raising the children fell squarely on her shoulders. As Dick later recalled, "She almost worked herself to death taking in washing to feed us."[51]

Era struggled to put food on the table, but love kept the family together. "We were poor," said Dick, "but being poor made us close."[52] The children helped out by doing chores on the family's small plot of land. When chores and homework were done, the boys spent their time playing ball on a nearby public field. All five were excellent athletes, especially shining in baseball and basketball. (Hank and Ron would both eventually join Dick in the major leagues.)

As a child, Dick was quiet and shy. "He was always real quiet," said his mother, "sensitive, the most sensitive of all my boys."[53] When he was seven years old, he was hit in the eye with a tin can. The injury caused his left eyelid to droop slightly, giving rise to his nickname of "Sleepy". It was not severe enough, however, to prevent him from carrying on the Allen family's sports legacy. Each one of the five brothers—Coy, Caesar, Hank, Dick,

---

White Sox manager Chuck Tanner (left) shares a lighthearted moment with star slugger Dick Allen. Allen is the only player in the history of the Chicago franchise to lead the American League in runs batted in.

and Ron—was All-State in basketball at Wampum High School. (When Coy was there, his chief rival was New Castle's Chuck Tanner, who became a close friend of the family and Dick's future manager with the White Sox.)

During Dick's years at Wampum, his exploits on the basketball court made him a local legend. In his senior year, as captain and starting guard, he led Wampum to the Class B state championship. As high school buddy Jim Santelli remembered, "This guy was the Magic Johnson of high school basketball back when the rest of us were taking one-hand set shots. Sleepy could stuff one hand, both hands, either hand. He could jump right through the roof. . . . He could have been NBA, if it wasn't for the fact that he could hit that little ball so far."[54]

Upon his graduation, Dick received basketball scholarship offers from dozens of colleges. His abilities as a power-hitting shortstop on the baseball team, however, had attracted the attention of several major-league scouts. John Ogden of the Philadelphia Phillies was the most persistent. Ogden was so eager to sign the youngster with what he called "muscles that can be seen rippling right through his uniform,"[55] he offered contracts to Dick's brothers Hank and Coy as well—Hank as a player and Coy as a scout. Dick agreed to a $60,000 contract, at the time the largest ever given to a black athlete. The Phillies assigned him to their Elmira (New York) farm team of the New York–Pennsylvania League where he began his pro career in 1960.

The Road to the Majors

Allen had a successful first season as a pro, batting .281 and stroking eight home runs. Although he performed well on the field, however, it was hard for the eighteen-year-old to adjust to life away from Wampum. His high telephone bill reflected his many calls home to his mother.

The next year, Allen shifted over to second base for Twin Falls in the Pioneer League. His production increased as he batted .317 and clouted twenty-one homers. He continued to climb the minor-league ladder in 1962, batting .329 for Williamsport. Allen hit twenty home runs and led the Eastern League with thirty-two doubles.

The Phillies were impressed with Allen's progress and promoted him to their Triple A International League farm club, the

Arkansas Travelers, who played their home games in the city of Little Rock, Arkansas. Afraid of the racial situation in a city that had been the scene of a memorable conflict over school desegregation in 1956, Allen asked the Phillies to reassign him to another team. When they refused, he staged a brief holdout. When he finally reported, his fears about Little Rock were confirmed. As the first black player to grace the team's roster, Allen was subjected to crank phone calls, signs such as "Let's not Negro-ize our baseball,"[56] and a threat against his life. He took out his bitterness on opposing pitchers and put together a solid year, leading the league in triples, home runs, runs batted in, and total bases.

The overall experience was a traumatic one for the twenty-one-year-old. Allen felt the Phillies had betrayed him. "When I was first told to go down there," he explained, "they told me I'd only have to stay thirty days, not the whole season. . . . They lied to me."[57] He later promised himself he would never again play for a team in the Deep South.

Rookie of the Year

The Phillies called Allen up to the big-league club at the tail end of the 1963 season. In his major-league debut, he batted .292 in ten games with seven hits and a pair of runs batted in. He would never again return to the minors.

The next year, Allen put together a solid rookie season. He pounded National League pitchers for a .318 batting average. Included among his 201 hits were 38 doubles, 13 triples (tied for the league lead), and 29 home runs (many of the tape-measure variety). He drove home 91 runs and led the circuit in runs scored with 125 and total bases with 352. In the field, he made 41 errors as he struggled playing third base, a new position for him.

Allen was rewarded for his impressive work by being named National League Rookie of the Year by both the Baseball Writers' Association and the *Sporting News*. Unfortunately, the Phillies struggled down the homestretch through one of baseball's most memorable collapses. With just twelve games left to play, they blew a six-and-a-half-game lead and finished in second place. Philadelphia fans and media, with a reputation as among the toughest in all sports, took out much of their frustration on Allen, ridiculing his fielding and making him a scapegoat for the club's late-season failures. (Ironically, he was honored by a group of fans with Richie Allen Night during the midst of the collapse.) Things would get worse in succeeding seasons.

The Frank Thomas Incident

Allen continued his slugging in the first half of 1965. By July 3, he was hitting a robust .348. During batting practice prior to the game that day, veteran outfielder Frank Thomas taunted him with a racial comment. (Thomas had a reputation for making insensitive remarks, and was not one of the best-liked players on the team.) Allen took a swing at Thomas. Thomas responded by swinging at Allen with his bat and hitting him on the left shoulder.

Frank Thomas surveys the waterlogged field after a game is called due to heavy rain. As teammates on the Philadelphia Phillies, Thomas and Allen were involved in an altercation that resulted in the release of Thomas from the team.

Following the game, the Phillies cut Thomas from the roster (a move they had been considering for a while), keeping the younger, more promising Allen instead. The fans, however, blamed Allen for Thomas's release. "When I showed my face the next night," he said in an interview for *Newsweek*, "the fans booed and threw things—and everything went downhill after that."[58] From that point on, Allen was viewed as a troublemaker by the fans and in the press. His performance dropped significantly the second half of the year. He finished the season with a .302 average, twenty home runs, and eighty-five runs batted in.

Wearing Out His Welcome

Allen set a Phillies' club record for right-handed hitters in 1966 when he blasted a career-high 40 home runs. He drove in 110 runs and led the league in slugging percentage with a mark of .632. He accomplished all this despite missing a month of the season due to a shoulder injury.

Allen's contract for 1967 called for a salary of $82,000, making him the highest-paid fourth-year player in major-league history. He continued his assault at the plate and made the All-Star team as the starting third baseman for the third time in four seasons. His home run helped the National League to a 2–1 victory in the summer classic.

A freak injury suffered on August 24 brought Allen's season to a premature end. While pushing a stalled car up a hill, he put his right hand through a headlight. Two tendons in the hand were cut and the ulnar nerve severed. A five-hour operation was required to repair the damage.

The Phillies tried to get Allen to sign a conditional contract for the next year to see if the injury hindered his performance. The move only served to embitter him. He was now determined to force a trade to another team. To do this, he became more and more of a disciplinary problem. He came late to games, missed batting practice, and showed up in no condition to play (drinking had become a way for him to escape from his problems). Allen incurred fines on more than one occasion. The team continued to put up with his actions, however, as long as he continued to produce with the bat. The injury did not hamper his slugging in 1968 (thirty-three homers, ninety runs batted in), but his average dropped to .263.

It did, however, hinder his throwing. Allen was moved from third base to the outfield where he became a target for fans throwing coins, bottles, and other objects. From that point on, he always wore a batting helmet for protection when he played the field.

Allen's problems in Philadelphia came to a head in 1969. The fans had become terribly abusive, smearing his car with paint, making crank phone calls, and tossing garbage on his lawn. Now playing first base, Allen answered their taunts by scratching out replies in the dirt with his foot. Although he still put up solid numbers (a .288 batting average, thirty-two home runs, and eighty-nine runs batted in), his actions were becoming more and more divisive. In late June, he was suspended indefinitely for missing a doubleheader in New York. Manager Gene Mauch had been fired in 1968 when the front office refused to discipline Allen to his satisfaction. Bob Skinner, Mauch's successor, eventually resigned when Philadelphia owner Bob Carpenter rescinded a $2,500 fine Skinner had administered when Allen missed an exhibition game near the end of the 1969 season. With the situation having reached the breaking point, Allen finally was traded to the St. Louis Cardinals.

New Starts

Allen began his stay in St. Louis on a positive note, hitting a home run on opening day in 1970. He finished the year with 34 round-trippers and 101 runs batted in despite missing more than a month due to a torn hamstring. The Cardinals finished a disappointing fourth in the National League and soon after the season ended, Allen was traded to the Dodgers. "I'd done everything expected of me," said Allen in his autobiography. "I worked hard . . . to keep team morale high. I kicked butt out on the diamond. I brought people into the park. . . . Clearly, I'd been labeled, blackballed. No amount of staying out of trouble was going to change what the baseball establishment thought of me."[59]

Los Angeles finished in second place in 1971, just two games out of first. Allen again had a solid year, batting .295 with twenty-three homers. He did not, however, totally buy into the team's glamorous Hollywood style. As he explained, "They put a lot of pressure on players to sign autographs and have their picture taken. They want you to visit with celebs in the clubhouse before games. . . . I kept telling these guys, un-uh, no, baby, I'm here to play ball, that other stuff is jive. It distracts from the team's mission to win ballgames."[60]

Soon after the season ended, Allen was sent on his way once again. This time, he was traded to the White Sox in exchange for pitcher Tommy John and infielder Steve Huntz.

The Savior

The White Sox were a struggling franchise when Allen joined the team. In the words of one Chicago writer, the 1972 team was one of "has beens and also rans."[61] Few people picked them to finish in the first division.

Chicago's manager was Chuck Tanner, Coy Allen's basketball rival from New Castle, Pennsylvania. Tanner was known as a "ballplayers' manager." He treated the players like men and cared only about winning. As long as the players showed up ready to play the game, he had no problem with them. For the first time in Allen's major-league career, he enjoyed coming to the

Allen loses his helmet as he slides into home plate. Allen's two and a half seasons with Chicago were the finest in his baseball career.

ballpark each day. "I feel more a part of this team than any other place I've been," he said. "There's a different feeling around here. In Philadelphia you play your heart out and if you come up a loser they really give it to you. Here the people make excuses for you if you lose. The guys around here are a lot easier to talk to without them getting mad or offended." [62]

Allen's performance in his first year with the White Sox is perhaps put into perspective best by his former manager. "In all my years of baseball," said Tanner, "I have never seen a season to compare to the one Dick Allen had in 1972. . . . He was on a rampage, a man on a mission. He could do anything he wanted. Dick Allen picked the White Sox up on his back and carried them all season. It was a powerful thing to watch." [63] All Allen did was lead the American League in home runs (37), runs batted in (113), walks (99), and slugging percentage (.603). He batted .308, scored 90 runs, stole 19 bases, and finished second among first basemen in fielding percentage. With Allen showing the way, the Sox finished in second place, just five games behind the Oakland A's. In the voting for the league's Most Valuable Player, he won in a landslide. His performance helped the club's attendance jump from just shy of 834,000 in 1971 to over 1,177,000 in 1972.

Following the season, Allen was rewarded with a new three-year contract calling for a salary of $250,000 per year, making him the highest-paid player in the game. When questioned about the contract, Chicago general manager Roland Hemond simply said, "Dick Allen is responsible for saving the Sox franchise. Period." [64]

Allen began 1973 intent on helping the team make another run at the pennant. Unfortunately, he suffered a hairline fracture of his leg in a collision with the Angels' Mike Epstein and had his year cut short. He still managed to connect for sixteen home runs and drive in forty-one runs in only seventy-two games, but things began to unravel. Some players resented what they considered special favors accorded to the Sox star. Many were also jealous of his exorbitant salary.

Allen returned at full strength in 1974 and proceeded to lead the league in home runs for a second time. A lingering shoulder injury and dissension on the team, however, caused him to announce his retirement from baseball in mid-September. Another page in the Dick Allen saga had come to an end.

Out to Pasture

Allen returned to his Pennsylvania farm where he intended to raise horses, another of his lifelong passions. Eventually, however, he decided he wanted to play again. He was signed by Philadelphia and played parts of two more seasons with the team.

The long layoff, however, had taken its toll. Allen was just a shell of his former self and was released by the Phillies following the 1976 season. He played fifty-four games in 1977 with the Oakland A's before hanging up his spikes for good. Since his retirement, Allen has spent a good deal of time indulging his love of horses and horse racing. In 1999 he took a job with the Philadelphia Phillies as a roving minor league instructor. He currently works in the team's community relations department.

Allen prepares to swing at a Nolan Ryan fastball. Allen retired from baseball as one of the best hitters in the sport.

Dick Allen retired with 351 career home runs, six All-Star appearances, and both Rookie of the Year and Most Valuable Player Awards to his credit. He most likely will never be elected to the Baseball Hall of Fame, but he will always be remembered for the way he played the game and the excitement he generated whenever he came to bat.

CHAPTER 7

Frank Thomas

Frank Thomas is unquestionably the most complete hitter to play for the White Sox since Joe Jackson. He is the only player in major-league history to bat .300 or better with twenty home runs, one hundred runs batted in, one hundred walks, and one hundred runs scored in seven consecutive seasons. Already on top of several Chicago career batting lists, he is a good bet to make the Hall of Fame when his playing days are over.

Destined for Stardom

Frank Edward Thomas Jr. was born on May 27, 1968, in Columbus, Georgia. He was the fifth of six children born to Frank and Charlie Mae Thomas. The couple had three daughters (Gloria, Mary, and Sharon) and a son (Michael) before Frank. They also had a younger daughter named Pamela to whom Frank became very close. Tragically, she died of leukemia when she was just two and a half years old. Some people believe his sister's death was one of the things that motivated Frank to become a great ballplayer.

Frank Sr. was a deacon at Nazareth Baptist Church and also a bail bondsman. His wife worked in a textile mill. Young Frank displayed a talent for sports at an early age. "I'm not bragging," said his father. "But Frank did so well in all sports. And he loved them all. I never crammed them down his throat. I never had to worry about him. It didn't matter what time of day or night it was, I knew Frank was at the Boys Club or the playground, somewhere with a ball in his hands."[65]

Frank loved basketball best, but excelled even more in baseball and football. Of his baseball skills, Frank Sr. said, "From the time he was in Little League he had a good eye. I always told him, 'Don't swing at bad pitches. Watch the ball all the way from the pitcher's hand to the plate.'"[66]

In Pop Warner football, Frank was a punishing tight end who leveled opponents with his devastating blocks. When the youngster was just nine years old, his coach, Chester Murray, told his father, "This kid will be a professional athlete. I don't know in what sport. But he *will be* a professional athlete."[67]

Frank Thomas looks on from the dugout during a 2002 game. Thomas is one of the most complete hitters in White Sox history.

Frank participated in all three sports at Columbus High School. He was a six-foot, four-inch forward in basketball who drew comparisons with Auburn University and National Basketball Association star Charles Barkley. He led the team in scoring and rebounding as a junior. In football he was a placekicking tight end who was courted by numerous colleges. He was eventually offered a scholarship to Auburn University.

By this point in time, however, baseball had become Frank's top priority. He hit .440 for the Blue Devils as a senior first baseman and dreamed of playing in the major leagues. Baseball scouts, however, believed he was committed to football at Auburn. Teams therefore ignored him in the June 1986 amateur draft. Shocked, Frank decided to accept the scholarship from Auburn.

"I'd hit .400 three straight years," he recalled, "and hit home run after home run for a team that won the state championship once and went to the finals two other years. . . . If I'd been drafted, I would have signed. I wanted to play baseball."[68]

A Tiger Legend

In Thomas's freshman year on coach Pat Dye's football squad at Auburn, he showed tremendous promise. He caught three passes for forty-five yards as a tight end, backing up Walter Reeves, who would later play six seasons in the National Football League. After suffering an injury in the third game of his sophomore year, however, Thomas decided to quit the sport to concentrate his energies on baseball. He carried with him a valuable lesson from his experiences on the gridiron. "Playing football at Auburn," he said, "was a whole new world for me. It made me a *man*. I had always thought I was working hard. But there, I learned what hard work means."[69]

For coach Hal Baird's baseball team, Thomas slugged a school single-season record twenty-one homers. His performance earned him a spot on *Baseball America*'s freshman All-America team. He followed up with two more outstanding years. After just three seasons, Thomas had already set a Tiger career record for home runs with forty-nine. He won the Southeastern Conference batting title two times and was named the conference's most valuable player in 1989. Thomas won a spot on the *Sporting News* All-America team that same season. As coach Baird told the *Chicago Tribune*, "He was the best we've ever had."[70]

Although he had an excellent year, Thomas had suffered another disappointment the previous year. He spent most of the summer of 1988 playing with the United States national baseball team that was preparing for the Seoul Summer Olympics. Despite hitting well over .300, however, Thomas did not make the squad. According to Team USA coach Mark Marquess, he was not invited because it was thought it would interfere with his football commitment to Auburn.

Despite this setback, Thomas was finally selected by a professional team in the June 1989 draft. He was taken by the White Sox with the seventh overall pick. In Thomas, Chicago saw a player who could help them in the near future. "Some scouts were down on him," said Sox general manager Larry Himes.

They looked at him as being strictly a DH-type [Designated Hitter] player; but we saw someone who would be able to play first base as well as give us the power we needed at the time. We also liked the fact that he scored high on our tests in the areas of poise, work habits, and intelligence. We figured he could get to the major leagues very quickly.[71]

Himes's assessment proved to be correct.

An Immediate Impact

Thomas began his pro career with the White Sox's Sarasota team in the Gulf Coast League in 1989, then moved up to the team's Class A club in the Florida State League. Between the two stops, he batted .288 with five home runs and forty-one runs batted in in only 236 trips to the plate.

Following a productive spring training in 1990, Thomas was sent to the White Sox' Double A farm team to work on his fielding. "We didn't want to have him be embarrassed defensively," said Himes. "We wanted him to be a complete player."[72] Although Thomas was frustrated at not making the big-league club, he went down and had an excellent season. He batted .323 with the Birmingham Barons, with eighteen home runs and seventy-one runs batted in. He continued to show an excellent eye at the plate by leading the league with 112 walks. For his efforts, *Baseball America* named him its Minor League Player of the Year.

That August, the Sox called Thomas up for his first taste of major-league action. Unlike many rookies, he was not intimidated by the prospect. Said Thomas, "A lot of guys when they get up here are overwhelmed by the big crowds, the TV, the media everywhere. It didn't bother me. I'd been around it at Auburn. Playing football in front of eighty thousand really helped."[73]

It did not take Thomas long to make his presence felt. In his big-league debut on August 2, he drove home the winning run. In sixty games over the last two months of the season, he batted .330 with seven homers and thirty-one runs batted in, and won Player of the Week honors in late September. His average was the highest by a White Sox player with at least two hundred plate appearances in forty-eight years. Thomas's performance was all the more

Thomas swings at a pitch during a 1991 game. That year marked the beginning of a series of very successful seasons for the Chicago slugger.

impressive since it came in the heat of a pennant race. The Sox finished the year in second place behind the Oakland A's. Although they had come up short in the race for the pennant, they found a player who would be the center of their offense for years to come.

The "Big Hurt"

The White Sox finished second again in 1991, but through no fault of Thomas's. The six-foot, five-inch, 240-pound slugger continued his stalwart hitting of the previous year. His .318 batting average led the team, as did his 178 hits, 104 runs, 31 doubles, 32 home runs, 109 runs batted in, and 138 walks (a franchise record). The walks also led the league, as did his .453 on-base percentage. All told, Thomas finished among the top ten players in the American League in nine offensive categories. He accomplished all this despite being hampered by a shoulder injury that limited him to duty as a designated hitter for much of the season.

Thomas came in third in the baseball writers' voting for the Most Valuable Player Award (behind Cal Ripken and Cecil Fielder). When the *New York Times* used a formula that took slugging percentage, on-base percentage, and salary into account, it concluded that he was the biggest bargain in baseball that season. Despite his unflagging confidence in his abilities, Thomas tried not to let his success go to his head. Above his locker were the letters D.B.T.H. to remind him "Don't Believe the Hype."

That was hard to do, since everyone was talking about him in spring training the next year. As sportswriter Thomas Boswell wrote, "If baseball has one player who'll be watched more closely than any other this season, it's Thomas. . . . When was the last time a player, after one full season, was widely considered the best hitter in baseball?"[74]

Thomas proceeded to fulfill everyone's expectations. He surpassed most of his previous season's marks in 1992, batting .323 with 185 hits, 108 runs scored, 46 doubles, and 115 runs batted in. For the second year in a row, he led the league in on-base percentage. His home run total dropped to 24, but his strikeouts also went down, from 112 to 88. It was also during the 1991 season that Thomas got his nickname. Seeing the way he consistently hammered the baseball, White Sox announcer and former major leaguer Ken Harrelson christened Thomas the "Big Hurt."

Most Valuable Player

By 1993, the White Sox were ready to make a strong run at a division title. They fulfilled their potential and won the American League West, coming in eight games ahead of the Texas Rangers. Jack McDowell led the league's best pitching staff, winning twenty-two games. The offense was dominated by Thomas. The Big Hurt paced the team with a .317 batting average, a White Sox–record 41 home runs, and 128 runs batted in. He continued showing patience at the plate by walking 112 times. Surprisingly, considering his increased home run total, he also reduced his strikeouts, fanning a total of just fifty-four times.

Thomas also joined a select group of players by becoming just the fifth man in history to bat over .300 with twenty home runs, 100 runs batted in, 100 runs scored, and 100 walks in three consecutive seasons. The other four players to accomplish the feat were Hall of Fame immortals Babe Ruth, Lou Gehrig, Jimmie Foxx, and Ted Williams. Amazingly, Thomas accomplished the feat by the time he was twenty-five years of age. (He would eventually post such impressive numbers an incredible seven years in a row.)

Despite Thomas's hitting heroics, he was just as pleased by the improvement he made in the field. As he told Steve Wulf of *Sports Illustrated*, "My favorite moment this year was a play I made at first. I dove to my right, then threw home to get the runner. I don't think I could have made that play before this year."[75] His all-around play earned him his first All-Star appearance at first base.

Although Thomas felt he had been slighted in the voting for the Most Valuable Player Award the previous two years, he would not be denied in 1993. Not only did he win the award, it

Thomas puts a ball into play in a 1993 game. The first baseman's strong offensive and defensive skills were recognized that year with the Most Valuable Player award.

was a unanimous selection for only the tenth time in baseball history. The only thing marring his season was the Sox's loss to the Toronto Blue Jays in the American League Championship Series (ALCS). Chicago lost in six games despite Thomas's .353 batting average.

Hall of Fame Numbers

Over the next four years, Thomas posted numbers of epic proportions. In 1994, the season was cut short because of a players' strike. In just 113 games, he batted .353 with 38 homers and 101 runs batted in. He led the league with 106 runs scored, 109 walks, and a .729 slugging percentage (the highest American League mark in thirty-seven years). The Sox were atop the newly formed Central Division at the time of the strike, which deprived them of perhaps their best chance at a pennant since 1959. For the second year in a row, Thomas was voted the league's Most Valuable Player.

The Sox contended over the next three seasons, but kept coming up short in their quest for a pennant. Thomas continued to put up staggering statistics as the one constant in the Sox offense. He clouted 40 home runs in both 1995 and 1996, and batted .349 with 134 runs batted in in the latter season. In 1997, he slugged 35 homers and drove in 125 runs while leading the American League in batting with a .347 average. In doing so, he became the first White Sox player to win the title since Luke Appling in 1943. Late that season, the White Sox rewarded him with a six-year, $85 million extension of his contract, assuring that he would remain in a Chicago uniform through 2006.

Thomas always had the utmost confidence in his abilities. By this point, he was beginning to seriously consider the possibility that he could someday make the Baseball Hall of Fame. "I've never understood why people say they don't think of the Hall of Fame," he said. "I want it. I'm not embarrassed to say that. I want to be the best."[76] The next two years, however, would throw some doubt on that possibility.

Hard Times

Although the White Sox finished in second place in 1997, their record was below .500 (80–81). Jerry Manuel took over as manager in 1998, at a time when Thomas's world was beginning to unravel. He and his wife separated, and a music business he'd invested in was struggling. The problems seemed to carry over onto the ball field. As former teammate Robin Ventura recalled, "He had that same passion and ability to focus, but now it was directed at something other than baseball: his music company. . . . Baseball didn't get that same level of attention."[77]

Thomas's batting average for 1998 was .265, the lowest mark of his career. He complained that umpires were calling pitches differently and that he had trouble adjusting to the expanded strike zone. Some of his teammates felt he was more concerned about his own stats than the interests of the team.

White Sox manager Jerry Manuel watches from the dugout during a 2002 game. Manuel has had a somewhat strained relationship with Thomas since becoming manager in 1998.

Things did not get much better in 1999. Injuries hampered Thomas's performance and played a part in causing a rift between him and Manuel. His manager wanted him to play first base, but Thomas insisted on being the designated hitter. His season became a series of complaints and excuses as his popularity among fans, teammates, and the media rapidly went downhill. Radio host Mike North of WSCR described Thomas as "the most unpopular superstar who ever played in Chicago. . . . Frank is a nice guy, but he's a whiner. He's a crybaby."[78]

The Comeback

The developing feud between Thomas and Manuel finally came to a head during spring training of 2000. Thomas's refusal to take part in a drill because of a foot injury ended up in a confrontation between the two men. After a two-hour closed-door meeting, Thomas and Manuel appeared to

Thomas congratulates a teammate who has just scored as he walks to the plate. Now in the twilight of his career, Thomas is struggling to achieve the level of play of his glory days.

have settled their differences. Thomas apologized to his teammates, explained about his foot injury, and told them, "I just want you to know I'm with you."[79]

Thomas proceeded to have one of the best seasons of his career in 2000. He batted .328 and reached career highs in home runs (43), runs batted in (143), runs scored (114), and hits (191). Following his lead, the White Sox raced to the Central Division title by compiling a league-high 95 wins. Their quest for a pennant, however, again ended in the Division Series. The Seattle Mariners swept Chicago in three games, holding Thomas hitless in nine at bats. Although disappointed, Thomas was satisfied that he had done all he could. "I gave what I had," he said, "and it just was not good enough."[80] His play was good enough, however, to see him finish second to Jason Giambi in the Most Valuable Player voting.

Thomas's six-day holdout over a contract squabble during spring training 2001 indicated that he still had a way to go to improve his image. He began the season slowly, then tore a tendon in his right arm in late April. He finished the year with a .221 batting average in just twenty games.

Whether Thomas can return to be the hitter he was earlier in his career remains to be seen. His desire to make the Hall of Fame someday continues to be a driving force. There can be little doubt, however, that during the decade of the 1990s, there was no better all-around hitter than the Big Hurt, Frank Thomas.

White Sox Achievements

White Sox Year-by-Year
Games

Year	W	L	Place	Back	Manager
1901	83	53	1st	+4	Griffith
1902	74	60	4th	8	Griffith
1903	60	77	7th	30$^1/_2$	Callahan
1904	89	65	3rd	6	Callahan, Jones
1905	92	60	2nd	2	Jones
1906	93	58	1st	+3	Jones
1907	87	64	3rd	5$^1/_2$	Jones
1908	88	64	3rd	1$^1/_2$	Jones
1909	78	74	4th	20	Sullivan
1910	68	85	6th	35$^1/_2$	Duffy
1911	77	74	4th	24	Duffy
1912	78	76	4th	28	Callahan
1913	78	74	5th	17$^1/_2$	Callahan
1914	70	84	6th*	30	Callahan
1915	93	61	3rd	9$^1/_2$	Rowland
1916	89	65	2nd	2	Rowland
1917	100	54	1st	+9	Rowland
1918	57	67	6th	17	Rowland
1919	88	52	1st	+3$^1/_2$	Gleason
1920	96	58	2nd	2	Gleason
1921	62	92	7th	36$^1/_2$	Gleason
1922	77	77	5th	17	Gleason
1923	69	85	7th	30	Gleason
1924	66	87	8th	25$^1/_2$	Evers
1925	79	75	5th	18$^1/_2$	Collins
1926	81	72	5th	9$^1/_2$	Collins
1927	70	83	5th	29$^1/_2$	Schalk
1928	72	82	5th	29	Schalk, Blackburne
1929	59	93	7th	46	Blackburne

Year	W	L	Place	Back	Manager
1930	62	92	7th	40	Bush
1931	58	97	8th	51	Bush
1932	49	102	7th	56½	Fonseca
1933	67	83	6th	31	Fonseca
1934	53	99	8th	47	Fonseca, Dykes
1935	74	78	5th	19½	Dykes
1936	81	70	3rd	20	Dykes
1937	86	68	3rd	16	Dykes
1938	65	83	6th	32	Dykes
1939	85	69	4th	22½	Dykes
1940	82	72	4th*	8	Dykes
1941	77	77	3rd	24	Dykes
1942	66	82	6th	34	Dykes
1943	82	72	4th	16	Dykes
1944	71	83	7th	18	Dykes
1945	71	78	6th	15	Dykes
1946	74	80	5th	30	Dykes
1947	70	84	6th	27	Lyons
1948	51	101	8th	44½	Lyons
1949	63	91	6th	34	Onslow
1950	60	94	6th	38	Onslow, Corriden
1951	81	73	4th	17	Richards
1952	81	73	3rd	14	Richards
1953	89	65	3rd	11½	Richards
1954	94	60	3rd	17	Richards, Marion
1955	91	63	3rd	5	Marion
1956	85	69	3rd	12	Marion
1957	90	64	2nd	8	Lopez
1958	82	72	2nd	10	Lopez
1959	94	60	1st	+5	Lopez
1960	87	67	3rd	10	Lopez
1961	86	76	4th	23	Lopez
1962	85	77	5th	11	Lopez
1963	94	68	2nd	10½	Lopez
1964	98	64	2nd	1	Lopez
1965	95	67	2nd	7	Lopez
1966	83	79	4th	15	Stanky
1967	89	73	4th	3	Stanky
1968	67	95	8th*	36	Stanky, Lopez

Year	W	L	Place	Back	Manager
1969	68	94	5th	29	Lopez, Gutteridge
1970	56	106	6th	42	Gutteridge, Tanner
1971	79	83	3rd	22½	Tanner
1972	87	67	2nd	5½	Tanner
1973	77	85	5th	17	Tanner
1974	80	80	4th	9	Tanner
1975	75	86	5th	22½	Tanner
1976	64	97	6th	25½	Richards
1977	90	72	3rd	12	Lemon
1978	71	90	5th	20½	Lemon, Doby
1979	73	87	5th	14	Kessinger, La Russa
1980	70	90	5th	26	La Russa
1981	54	52	3rd/6th**	—	La Russa
1982	87	75	3rd	6	La Russa
1983	99	63	1st***	+20	La Russa
1984	74	88	5th*	10	La Russa
1985	85	77	3rd	6	La Russa
1986	72	90	5th	20	La Russa, Fregosi
1987	77	85	5th	8	Fregosi
1988	71	90	5th	32½	Fregosi
1989	89	92	7th	29½	Torborg
1990	94	68	2nd	9	Torborg
1991	87	75	2nd	8	Torborg
1992	86	76	3rd	10	Lamont
1993	94	68	1st***	+8	Lamont
1994	67	46	1st	+1	Lamont
1995	68	76	3rd	32	Lamont, Bevington
1996	85	77	2nd****	14½	Bevington
1997	80	81	2nd	6	Bevington
1998	80	82	2nd	9	Manuel
1999	75	86	2nd	21½	Manuel
2000	95	67	1st	+5	Manuel
2001	83	79	3rd	8	Manuel

*Tied for position.
**First half 31–22, second half 23–30.
***Lost Championship Series.
****Lost division playoff.

A.L. MVPs

Nellie Fox, 2B	1959
Dick Allen, 1B	1972
Frank Thomas, 1B	1993
Frank Thomas, 1B	1994

Cy Young Winners

Early Wynn, RH	1959
LaMarr Hoyt, RH	1983
Jack McDowell, RH	1993

Rookies of the Year

Luis Aparicio, SS	1956
Gary Peters, P	1963
Tommie Agee, OF	1966
Ron Kittle, OF	1983
Ozzie Guillen, SS	1985

Managers of the Year

Tony La Russa	1983
Jeff Torborg	1990
Gene Lamont	1993
Jerry Manuel	2000

A.L. Home Run Champions

1971—Bill Melton	33
1972—Dick Allen	37
1974—Dick Allen	32

A.L. RBI Champions

1972—Dick Allen	113

A.L. Batting Champions

1936—Luke Appling	.388
1943—Luke Appling	.328
1997—Frank Thomas	.347

A.L. ERA Champions

1906—Doc White	1.52
1907—Ed Walsh	1.60
1910—Ed Walsh	1.27
1917—Ed Cicotte	1.53
1921—Red Faber	2.48
1922—Red Faber	2.80
1941—Thornton Lee	2.37
1942—Ted Lyons	2.10
1947—Joe Haynes	2.42
1951—Saul Rogovin	2.48*
1955—Billy Pierce	1.97
1960—Frank Baumann	2.67
1963—Gary Peters	2.33
1966—Gary Peters	1.98
1967—Joel Horlen	2.06

*ERA compiled with two teams

A.L. Strikeout Champions

1908—Ed Walsh	269
1909—Frank Smith	177
1911—Ed Walsh	255
1953—Billy Pierce	186
1958—Early Wynn	179

Stolen Bases

Year-by-Year Leaders

American League	SB	Year
Frank Isbell	52	1901
Patsy Dougherty	47	1908
Eddie Collins	33	1919
Eddie Collins	48	1923

American League	SB	Year
Eddie Collins	42	1924
Johnny Mostil	43	1925
Johnny Mostil	35	1926
Minnie Minoso	31	1951
Minnie Minoso	22	1952
Minnie Minoso	25	1953
Luis Aparicio	21	1956
Luis Aparicio	28	1957
Luis Aparicio	29	1958
Luis Aparicio	56	1959
Luis Aparicio	51	1960
Luis Aparicio	53	1961
Luis Aparicio	31	1962

Notes

Introduction: Second-Class Citizens in the Second City

1. Quoted in Bob Vanderberg, *Sox: From Lane to Fain to Zisk and Fisk*. Chicago, IL: Chicago Review Press, 1984, p. xi.

Chapter 1: The Comiskey Curse

2. Quoted in Richard C. Lindberg, *The White Sox Encyclopedia*. Philadelphia, PA: Temple University Press, 1997, p. 6.
3. Quoted in Geoffrey C. Ward and Ken Burns, *Baseball: An Illustrated History*. New York: Alfred A. Knopf, 1994, p. 144.
4. Quoted in Lindberg, *White Sox Encyclopedia*, p. 57.
5. Quoted in Lindberg, *White Sox Encyclopedia*, p. 69.
6. Quoted in Larry Kalas, *Strength Down the Middle*. Chicago, IL: RR Donnelley & Sons, 1999, p. 186.
7. Quoted in Lindberg, *White Sox Encyclopedia*, p. 74.

Chapter 2: Joe Jackson

8. Quoted in David L. Fleitz, *Shoeless*. Jefferson, NC: McFarland & Company, 2001, p. 12.
9. Quoted in Fleitz, *Shoeless*, p. 17.
10. Quoted in Fleitz, *Shoeless*, p. 22.
11. Quoted in Fleitz, *Shoeless*, p. 37.
12. Quoted in David Pietrusza, Matthew Silverman, and Michael Gershman, eds., *Baseball: The Biographical Encyclopedia*. New York: Total/Sports Illustrated, 2000, p. 548.
13. Quoted in Fleitz, *Shoeless*, p. 232.
14. Quoted in Fleitz, *Shoeless*, p. 261.
15. Quoted in Fleitz, *Shoeless*, p. 266.
16. Quoted in "Joe Jackson," *Baseball Library.Com*, www.pubdim.net/baseballlibrary.
17. Quoted in Fleitz, *Shoeless*, p. 275.

Chapter 3: Nellie Fox

18. Quoted in David Gough and Jim Bard, *Little Nel: The Nellie Fox Story.* Bend, OR: Maverick Publications, 2000, p. 14.
19. Quoted in Charles Moritz, ed., *Current Biography Yearbook: 1960.* New York: H. W. Wilson, 1960, p. 150.
20. Quoted in Gough and Bard, *Little Nel,* p. 16.
21. Quoted in Gough and Bard, *Little Nel,* p. 20.
22. Quoted in Moritz, *Current Biography Yearbook: 1960,* p. 150.
23. Quoted in Lindberg, *White Sox Encyclopedia,* p. 154.
24. Quoted in Gough and Bard, *Little Nel,* p. 33.
25. Quoted in Gough and Bard, *Little Nel,* p. 79.
26. Quoted in Moritz, *Current Biography Yearbook: 1960,* p. 150.
27. Quoted in Gough and Bard, *Little Nel,* p. 87.
28. Quoted in Moritz, *Current Biography Yearbook: 1960,* p. 150.
29. Quoted in Gough and Bard, *Little Nel,* p. 193.
30. Quoted in Gough and Bard, *Little Nel,* p. 243.
31. Quoted in David Gough, "Nellie Fox," *Baseball Research Journal: 1997* (1997): 113.

Chapter 4: Minnie Minoso

32. Quoted in Pietrusza, Silverman, and Gershman, *Baseball,* p. 786.
33. Quoted in Minnie Minoso with Herb Fagen, *Just Call Me Minnie: My Six Decades in Baseball.* Champaign, IL: Sagamore Publishing, 1994, p. 10.
34. Quoted in Minoso with Fagen, *Just Call Me Minnie,* p. 20.
35. Quoted in Minoso with Fagen, *Just Call Me Minnie,* p. 26.
36. Quoted in Richard C. Lindberg, "Minoso by Any Other Name," *National Pastime: 1992* (1992): 56.
37. Quoted in Minoso with Fagen, *Just Call Me Minnie,* p. 48.
38. Quoted in Vanderberg, *Sox,* p. 151.
39. Quoted in Pietrusza, Silverman, and Gershman, *Baseball,* p. 787.

Chapter 5: Bill Veeck

40. Quoted in Bill Veeck with Ed Linn, *Veeck—As in Wreck.* New York: Bantam Books, 1963, p. 16.
41. Quoted in Pietrusza, Silverman, and Gershman, *Baseball,* p. 1,165.

42. Quoted in Veeck with Linn, *Veeck,* p. 26.
43. Quoted in Pietrusza, Silverman, and Gershman, *Baseball,* p. 1,165.
44. Quoted in Anna Rothe, ed., *Current Biography Yearbook: 1948.* New York: H. W. Wilson, 1948, p. 646.
45. Quoted in Vanderberg, *Sox,* p. 21.
46. Quoted in Vanderberg, *Sox,* p. 24.
47. Quoted in Lindberg, *White Sox Encyclopedia,* p. 318.
48. Quoted in Vanderberg, *Sox,* p. 29.
49. Quoted in Vanderberg, *Sox,* p. 37.
50. Quoted in Bob Chieger, ed., *Voices of Baseball.* New York: New American Library, 1983, p. 129.

Chapter 6: Dick Allen

51. Quoted in Charles Moritz, ed., *Current Biography Yearbook: 1973.* New York: H. W. Wilson, 1973, p. 4.
52. Quoted in Moritz, *Current Biography Yearbook: 1973,* p. 4.
53. Quoted in Dick Allen and Tim Whitaker, *Crash: The Life and Times of Dick Allen.* New York: Ticknor & Fields, 1989, p. 51.
54. Quoted in Allen and Whitaker, *Crash,* p. 38.
55. Quoted in Allen and Whitaker, *Crash,* p. 47.
56. Quoted in Edward Kiersh, *Where Have You Gone, Vince DiMaggio?* New York: Bantam Books, 1983, p. 200.
57. Quoted in Kiersh, *Where Have You Gone?* p. 201.
58. Quoted in Moritz, *Current Biography Yearbook: 1973,* p. 5.
59. Quoted in Allen and Whitaker, *Crash,* p. 131.
60. Quoted in Allen and Whitaker, *Crash,* p. 134.
61. Quoted in Allen and Whitaker, *Crash,* p. 138.
62. Quoted in Lindberg, *White Sox Encyclopedia,* p. 112.
63. Quoted in Allen and Whitaker, *Crash,* p. 139.
64. Quoted in Allen and Whitaker, *Crash,* p. 148.

Chapter 7: Frank Thomas

65. Quoted in Steve Rushin, "No Doubting Thomas," *Sports Illustrated,* September 16, 1991, p. 32.
66. Quoted in Paul Ladewski, "Big Hurt," *Inside Sports,* March 1992, p. 48.
67. Quoted in Rushin, "No Doubting Thomas," p. 32.

68. Quoted in Judith Graham, ed., *Current Biography Yearbook: 1994.* New York: H. W. Wilson, 1994, p. 594.
69. Quoted in Johnette Howard, "Frankly Speaking," *Sport,* April 1992, p. 43.
70. Quoted in Graham, *Current Biography Yearbook: 1994,* p. 594.
71. Quoted in Ladewski, "Big Hurt," p. 49.
72. Quoted in Ladewski, "Big Hurt," p. 49.
73. Quoted in Graham, *Current Biography Yearbook: 1994,* p. 595.
74. Quoted in Graham, *Current Biography Yearbook: 1994,* p. 595.
75. Quoted in Graham, *Current Biography Yearbook: 1994,* p. 595.
76. Quoted in "Frank Thomas," *Baseball Library.Com,* www.pub dim.net/baseballlibrary.
77. Quoted in William Nack, "Hurtin'," *Sports Illustrated,* March 13, 2000, p. 71.
78. Quoted in Nack, "Hurtin'," p. 74.
79. Quoted in Nack, "Hurtin'," p. 68.
80. Quoted in "Frank Thomas," *Baseball Library.Com.*

For Further Reading

Books

Craig Carter and Dave Sloan, eds., *The Sporting News Baseball Guide: 1999 Edition*. St. Louis, MO: The Sporting News, 1999. The ultimate reference guide for the 1999 baseball season.

Jordan A. Deutsch, Richard M. Cohen, Roland T. Johnson, and David S. Neft, *The Scrapbook History of Baseball*. Indianapolis, IN: Bobbs-Merrill, 1975. This 320-page work covers one hundred years of baseball through a collection of historic newspaper accounts.

Steve Fiffer, *Speed*. Alexandria, VA: Redefinition, 1990. This lavishly illustrated volume in the World of Baseball series gives a detailed look at the effects speed has on the national pastime.

Bill James, *The New Bill James Historical Baseball Abstract*. New York: Simon & Schuster, 2001. This revised edition of the 1985 classic describes the evolution of the sport of baseball over the decades.

Lawrence T. Lorimer, *Baseball Desk Reference*. New York: DK Publishing, 2002. This comprehensive volume of over six hundred pages was written in collaboration with the National Baseball Hall of Fame and Museum.

Works Consulted

Books

Dick Allen and Tim Whitaker, *Crash: The Life and Times of Dick Allen*. New York: Ticknor & Fields, 1989. The autobiography of one of baseball's most controversial and colorful superstars.

Bob Chieger, ed., *Voices of Baseball*. New York: New American Library, 1983. A collection of quotations about baseball topics ranging from baserunning to umpires.

David L. Fleitz, *Shoeless*. Jefferson, NC: McFarland & Company, 2001. The definitive biography of one of the greatest hitters in baseball history.

David Gough and Jim Bard, *Little Nel: The Nellie Fox Story*. Bend, OR: Maverick Publications, 2000. The biography of the White Sox Hall of Fame second baseman.

Judith Graham, ed., *Current Biography Yearbook: 1994*. New York: H. W. Wilson, 1994. A library volume that contains all of the biographies published in *Current Biography* magazine in 1994.

Larry Kalas, *Strength Down the Middle*. Chicago, IL: RR Donnelley & Sons, 1999. The story of the 1959 pennant-winning Go-Go White Sox.

Edward Kiersh, *Where Have You Gone, Vince DiMaggio?* New York: Bantam Books, 1983. A collection of portraits of fifty-six former major leaguers from the 1950s and 1960s.

Richard C. Lindberg, *The White Sox Encyclopedia*. Philadelphia, PA: Temple University Press, 1997. This voluminous work of 570 pages includes a year-by-year history of the team and profiles of former players and managers.

Minnie Minoso with Herb Fagen, *Just Call Me Minnie: My Six Decades in Baseball*. Champaign, IL: Sagamore Publishing, 1994. The biography of one of the most exciting players of the 1950s.

Charles Moritz, ed., *Current Biography Yearbook: 1960.* New York: H. W. Wilson, 1960. A library volume that contains all of the biographies published in *Current Biography* magazine in 1960.

————, *Current Biography Yearbook: 1973.* New York: H. W. Wilson, 1973. A library volume that contains all of the biographies published in *Current Biography* magazine in 1973.

David Pietrusza, Matthew Silverman, and Michael Gershman, eds., *Baseball: The Biographical Encyclopedia.* New York: Total/ Sports Illustrated, 2000. This volume contains brief biographies of over two thousand players, managers, umpires, and front office figures from the national pastime's glorious history.

Anna Rothe, ed., *Current Biography Yearbook: 1948.* New York: H. W. Wilson, 1948. A library volume that contains all of the biographies published in *Current Biography* magazine in 1948.

Bob Vanderberg, *Sox: From Lane to Fain to Zisk and Fisk.* Chicago, IL: Chicago Review Press, 1984. This history of the White Sox from the late 1940s through the 1970s includes interviews with many former Chicago players.

Bill Veeck with Ed Linn, *Veeck—As in Wreck.* New York: Bantam Books, 1963. The autobiography of baseball's greatest promoter.

Geoffrey C. Ward and Ken Burns, *Baseball: An Illustrated History.* New York: Alfred A. Knopf, 1994. A beautifully illustrated history of the national pastime to accompany the television series.

Periodicals

David Gough, "Nellie Fox," *Baseball Research Journal: 1997* (1997).

Johnette Howard, "Frankly Speaking," *Sport,* April 1992.

Paul Ladewski, "Big Hurt," *Inside Sports,* March 1992.

Richard C. Lindberg, "Minoso by Any Other Name," *National Pastime: 1992* (1992).

William Nack, "Hurtin'," *Sports Illustrated,* March 13, 2000.

Steve Rushin, "No Doubting Thomas," *Sports Illustrated*, September 16, 1991.

Internet Sources

"Frank Thomas," *Baseball Library.Com.* www.pubdim.net/baseball library.

"Joe Jackson," *Baseball Library.Com.* www.pubdim.net/baseball library.

Index

Picture Credits

About the Author

John F. Grabowski is a native of Brooklyn, New York. He holds a bachelor's degree in psychology from City College of New York and a master's degree in educational psychology from Teacher's College, Columbia University. He has been a teacher for thirty-three years, as well as a freelance writer, specializing in the fields of sports, education, and comedy. His body of published work includes thirty-eight books; a nationally syndicated sports column; consultation on several math textbooks; articles for newspapers, magazines, and the programs of professional sports teams; and comedy material sold to Jay Leno, Joan Rivers, Yakov Smirnoff, and numerous other comics. He and his wife, Patricia, live in Staten Island with their daughter, Elizabeth.